Vest Pocket
SPANISH

Formerly published as: SPANISH IN A NUTSHELL

By
DR. SUSANA REDONDO
Assistant Professor of Spanish
Columbia University

PUBLISHED BY
INSTITUTE FOR LANGUAGE STUDY
Montclair, New Jersey 07042

DISTRIBUTED TO THE BOOK TRADE BY
BARNES & NOBLE BOOKS
A DIVISION OF HARPER & ROW, *PUBLISHERS*

Library of Congress Catalog Card Number: 58-8918

ISBN 0-8489-5001-1 (Paperbound)

ISBN 0-8489-5051-8 (Hardcover)

Printed in the United States of America

9 8 7 6 5 4 3 2 1

GETTING THE MOST OUT OF YOUR COURSE

THE WORLD is growing smaller every day. Far-sighted people who recognize the value of speaking a second language will reap the benefits of greater business success, more traveling enjoyment, easier study and finer social relationships.

VEST POCKET SPANISH will unlock for you the treasure house of learning a language the easy way, with a fresh, new approach—without monotonous drills. Before you know it, you'll be speaking your new language easily and without embarrassment. You will be able to converse with fascinating people from other lands and read books and magazines from their country in the original language.

Much research and painstaking study has gone into the "Vest Pocket" method of learning a new language as easily as possible. This Course is the result of that research, and for the reader's convenience it is divided into several basic, closely related sections:

The KEY TO PRONUNCIATION explains the sounds of the language. Each sentence is accompanied by the phonetic spelling to help you learn the pronunciation. This method has been tested extensively and is found to be the best to enable the student to associate sounds with written forms.

The BASIC SENTENCE PATTERNS are the unique new approach to sentence construction. Here you will find sentence patterns needed in general conversation. On these basic patterns you can build sentences to suit your own particular needs.

The EVERYDAY CONVERSATIONS form the main section of this book. Here you will find a large number of situations useful for general language learning and traveling purposes. You will learn hundreds upon hundreds of conversational sentences you may need to make yourself understood. Even more important, the material is organized to provide you with a wide basis for varying the vocabulary and sentences as much as your interest and ingenuity might desire.

The OUTLINE OF GRAMMAR provides a rapid understanding of the grammatical structure of your new language. The "Basic Sentence Patterns" are closely correlated with this section to give you a quick knowledge of the language.

The two-way DICTIONARY of over 6500 entries includes all the words used in the Everyday Conversations and contains another 3000 frequently used words and expressions. It thus forms a compact and invaluable tool for the student.

Here are the tools. Use them systematically, and before you know it you will have a "feeling" for the new language. The transcriptions furnish authentic reproduction of the language to train your ear and tongue to the foreign sounds; thus you can SEE the phrase, SAY the phrase, HEAR the phrase, and LEARN the phrase.

Remember that repetition and practice are the foundation stones of language learning. Repeat and practice what you have learned as often as you can. You will be amazed (and your friends will, too) how quickly you have acquired a really practical knowledge of Spanish.

THE EDITORS

TABLE OF CONTENTS

Getting the Most out of your Course   3

Key to Spanish Pronunciation   7

Basic Sentence Patterns   8

Everyday Conversations   17

    Basic Expressions   17
    Getting to Know You   18
    Counting   20
    The Clock and the Calendar   21
    Stranger in Town   23
    Aboard Ship   26
    Plane Travel   27
    All Aboard   29
    Going through Customs   30
    Taxi!   31
    Bus Stop   32
    Motoring through Latin America   33
    At the Hotel   34
    Renting a Room   37
    The Sidewalk Café   38
    Dining Out   39
    Native Dishes   41
    Sightseeing and Amusements   43
    Snapshots for Remembrance   47
    Shopping with Assurance   49
    Laundry and Cleaning   54
    Hairdressers and Barbers   54
    Going to Church   55

Theater Going   5(

Night Life   5(

Exchanging Money   5'

Communications (Mail, Telephoning, Telegrams)   58

Tourist Information   61

Your Health Abroad   62

Sports   63

Conducting Business   64

Outline of Spanish Grammar   6!

   1. The Article   6!

   2. The Noun   6.

   3. The Adjective   6(

   4. The Pronoun   6

   5. The Numerals   7

   6. The Preposition   7

   7. The Adverb   7

   8. The Conjunction   7:

   9. The Interjection   7:

  10. The Verb   7

Table of Irregular Verbs   7

Useful Information for Motorists   8

Spanish—English Dictionary   8

English—Spanish Dictionary   10(

KEY TO SPANISH PRONUNCIATION

Spanish sounds are easy to master. There are only five vowel sounds:

SPANISH SPELLING	PHONETIC SYMBOL	DESCRIPTION	EXAMPLES
a	ah	as in *father*	*butaca* (boo-tah'kah) , armchair
e	ay	as in *met*	*mesa* (may'sah) , table
i	ee	as in *machine*	*primo* (pree'moh) , cousin
o	oh	as in *north*	*esposo* (ays-poh'soh) , husband
u	oo	as in *rule*	*duda* (doo'dah) , doubt

Spanish diphthongs are common, but their pronunciation offers no difficulty, since each of the two vowels keeps its individual quality even though both are pronounced in conjunction *bueno* (booay'noh) good; *caigo* (kah'ee-goh) I fall; *pausa* (pah'oo-sah) pause; *miente* (meeayn'tay) mind; *reina* (ray'ee-nah) queen; *oigo* (oh'ee-goh) I hear; *feudo* (fay'oo-doh) feud.

The consonants *d, f, l, m, n, p, q, s, t, x,* and *ch* are pronounced almost as in English.

C is pronounced as *k* in *key* before *a, o, u,* or before a consonant and *s* as in *see* (in Latin American Spanish) or *th* as in *thin* (in Castilian Spanish) before e and i: *cada* (kah'dah) , each; *cena* (say'nah) , supper; *cruz* (kroos) , cross.

G as *g* in *go* before *a, o, u,* or before a consonant, and as *h* in *hue,* before *e* and *i*: *gato* (gah'toh) , cat; *gente* (hayn'tay) , people.

H is never pronounced: *hacer* (ah-sayr') , to do.

J as *h* in *hue*: *jugar* (hoo-gahr') , to play.

LL as *y* in *yes* (in Latin-American Spanish) or as *lli* in *billiards* (in Castilian Spanish) : *calle* (kah'yay or kah'lyay) , street.

N as *ny* in *canyon*: *niño* (nee'nyoh) , child.

R (as *r* in British *very*) is a trilled *r*: *pero* (pay'roh) , but.

RR as single Spanish *r*, but much more strongly trilled: *perro* (pay'rroh) dog.

Y as *y* in *yes*: *yo* (yoh) I.

Z as *s* in *see* (in Latin-American Spanish) or as *th* in *thin* (in Castilian Spanish) : *zapato* (sah-pah'toh *or* thah-pah'toh) , shoe.

B and **V** are pronounced alike, but they have two different pronunciations depending on their position. At the beginning of a word and after *m* or *n*, they are pronounced as *b* in *Bob*. In all other cases, they are pronounced as *v* but with the lips brought together: *bobo* (boh'boh) fool; *breve* (bray'vay) brief; *vaca* (vah'kah) cow; *vivir* (vee-veer') to live.

The **accent** of the words is indicated in the phonetic transcription of the phrases by an accent mark following the syllable to be stressed.

The rules concerning the position of the accent in Spanish are: All words ending in a vowel, in *n* or in *s* have the accent on the next to the last syllable. In all other cases the accent is on the last syllable, except when it is marked by an accent in the spelling of a word.

BASIC SENTENCE PATTERNS

In each language there are a few basic types of sentences which are used more often than others in everyday speech.

On the basis of such sentences, it is possible to form many others by substituting one or two of the words of each of these basic sentences. The sentences selected to illustrate the basic patterns are short, easy to memorize and useful. Learning them before you tackle the main section of the book with the phrases which cover everyday needs and travel situations, you will acquire an idea of the structure of the language. You will also learn indirectly through these basic types of sentences some of the most important grammatical categories and their function in the construction of the sentences the natural way—the way they are encountered in actual usage.

Cross references have been supplied to establish a correlation between the basic sentence patterns and the Grammar section in this book. This will help you to relate the grammatical knowledge you'll acquire passively going through the sentences to the systematic presentation of the basic facts of grammar. For example, when you encounter the phrase "See 4.4" in the first group of sentences, it means that by turning to chapter 4, subdivision 4 in the Grammar section you will find a description of the interrogative pronouns and their uses.

SIMPLE QUESTIONS AND ANSWERS
(See 4.4; 4.1; 2.1-2; 4.3)

¿Quién es él?
keeayn' ays ayl?
Who is he?

Es mi padre (tío, abuelo).
ays mee pah'dray (tee'oh, ah-booay'loh).
He is my father (uncle, grandfather).

¿Quién es ella?
keeayn' ays ay'yah?
Who is she?

Es mi madre (tía, abuela).
ays mee mah'dray (tee'ah, ah-booay'lah).
She is my mother (aunt, grandmother).

¿Quién es ese muchacho?
keeayn' ays ay'say moo-chah'choh?
Who is that boy?

Es mi hermano (primo, sobrino).
ays mee ayr-mah'noh (pree'moh, soh-bree'noh).
He is my brother (cousin, nephew).

8

¿Quién es el otro muchacho?
keeayn' ays ayl oh'troh moo-chah'choh?
Who is the other boy?

Ése es mi hermano mayor.
ay'say ays mee ayr-mah'noh mah-yohr'.
That's my older brother.

¿Quién es esa muchacha?
keeayn' ays ay'sah moo-chah'chah?
Who is that girl?

Es mi hermana menor (prima, sobrina).
ays mee ayr-mah'nah may-nohr' (pree'mah, soh-bree'nah).
She is my younger sister (cousin, niece).

¿Quiénes son ellos?
keeay'nays sohn ay'yohs?
Who are they?

Son mis abuelos.
sohn mees ah-booay'lohs.
They are my grandparents.

Esa muchacha alta es mi amiga. (See 4.5)
ay'sah moo-chah'chah ahl'tah ays mee ah-mee'gah.
That tall girl is my friend.

¿De veras? (¿Es verdad?)
day vay'rahs? (ays vayr-dahd'?)
Is that so?

¿Dónde está mi sombrero? (See 7.4)
dohn'day ays-tah' mee sohm-bray'roh?
Where is my hat?

Aquí está.
ah-kee' ays-tah'.
Here it is.

¿(En) dónde está su portafolio?
(ayn) dohn'day ays-tah' soo pohr-tah-foh'leeoh?
Where is your briefcase?

Está allí.
ays-tah' ah-yee'.
It's over there.

¿Dónde está su cartera (de ella)?
dohn-day ays-tah' soo kahr-tay'rah (day ay'yah)?
Where's her handbag?

Está aquí.
ays-tah' ah-kee'.
It's over here.

¿(En) dónde está el baño? (cuarto para señoras . . . caballeros?)
*(ayn) dohn'day ays-tah' ayl bah'nyoh? (kwahr'toh pah'rah
say-nyoh'rahs . . . kah-bah-yay'rohs?)*
Where's the washroom?

Está a la derecha (a la izquierda).
ays-tah' ah lah day-ray'chah (ah lah ees-keeayr'dah).
It's on the right (on the left).

¿(En) dónde está el cuarto de Juan? (See 2.3)
(ayn) dohn'day ays-tah' ayl kwahr'toh day hooahn'.
Where is John's room?

Está por allá derecho.
ays-tah' pohr ah-yah' day-ray' choh.
It's straight ahead.

¿(En) dónde está el cuarto de María?
(ayn) dohn'day ays-tah' ayl kwahr'toh day mah-ree'ah?
Where is Mary's room?

Está un piso más arriba.
ays-tah' oon pee'soh mahs ah-rree'bah.
It's one flight up.

QUESTIONS WITH *WHO* AND *WHOM*
(Interrogatives and Demonstratives; See 4.1, 4.3-5)

¿Quién tiene mis cuadernos? Pablo los tiene.
keeayn' teeay'nay mees kwah-dayr'nohs? Pah'bloh lohs teeay'nay.
Who has my notebooks? Paul has them.

¿Con quién hablaba usted? Con mi amigo Pedro.
koon keeayn' ah-blah'bah oos-tayd'? koon mee ah-mee'goh pay'droh.
With whom were you talking? With my friend Peter.

¿Quiénes son esos hombres? Son los amigos de mi hijo.
keeay'nays sohn ay'sohs ohm'brays?
Sohn lohs ah-mee'gohs day mee ee'hoh.
Who are those men? They are my son's friends.

¿Quiénes son esas muchachas? Son las condiscípulas de mi hija.
keeay'nays sohn ay'sahs moo-chah'chahs?
Sohn lahs kohn-dees-see'poo-lahs day mee ee-hah.
Who are those girls? They are my daughter's schoolmates.

¿Qué dijo ella? Dijo que no pudo venir.
kay' dee-hoh ay'yah? Dee'hoh kay noh poo'doh vay-neer'.
What did she say? She said she couldn't come.

¿En qué trabaja usted? Soy vendedor.
ayn kay trah-bah'hah oos-tayd'? sohy vayn-day-dohr'.
What is your occupation? I am a salesman.

¿Qué es amor? Es una cosa maravillosa.
kay ays ah-mohr'? ays oo'nah koh'sah mah-rah-vee-yoh'sah.
What is love? It's a wonderful thing.

¿Cuál de estos libros le gusta más? Éste.
kwahl day ays'tohs lee'brohs lay goos'tah mahs? ays'tay.
Which one of these books do you like best? This one.

SENTENCES WITH *HIM, HER* AND *IT*
(*Personal Object Pronouns*; See 4.1; 10.2, 10.4)

Juan se lo dió (a él).
hooahn' say loh deeoh (ah ayl).
John gave it to him.

Él me lo dió (a mí).
ayl may loh deeoh' (ah mee').
He gave it to me.

Yo se lo di (a ella).
yoh say loh dee' (ah ay'yah).
I gave it to her.

Ella nos lo envió.
ay'yah nohs loh ayn-veeoh'.
She sent it to us.

(Nosotros) se lo dimos (a usted).
(noh-soh'trohs) say loh dee'mohs (ah oos-tayd').
We gave it to you.

Usted no se lo dió (a ellos).
oos-tayd' noh say loh deeoh' (ah ay'yohs).
You did not give it to them.

Démelo.
day'may-loh.
Give it to me.

No se lo dé (a él).
noh say loh day (ah ayl).
Don't give it to him.

Envíeselo (a ella).
ayn-vee'ay-say-loh (ah ay'yah).
Send it to her.

Mándenoslo por correo.
mahn'-day-nohs'loh pohr koh-rray'oh.
Mail it to us.

No se lo envíe por correo (a ellos).
noh say loh ayn-vee'ay pohr koh-rray'oh (ah ay'yohs).
Don't mail it to them.

SENTENCES ON THE USE OF *THE, AN* AND *A*
(*The Article*; See 1.1-5; especially 1.3, 1.5)

El tenedor, la cuchara, los cuchillos y las cucharitas están sobre la mesa.
*ayl tay-nay-dohr', lah koo-chah'rah, lohs koo-chee'yohs ee lahs
    koo-chah-ree'tahs ays-tahn' soh'bray lah may-sah.*
The fork, the spoon, the knives and the teaspoons are on the table.

Me compré una cama, unas sillas, un sillón y unos espejos.
may kohm-bray' oo'nah kah'mah, oo'nahs see'yahs, oon see-yohn' ee
oo'nohs ays-pay' hohs.
I bought a bed, some chairs, an armchair and some mirrors.

Ellos viven en la Tercera Avenida.
ay-yohs vee-vayn ayn lah tayr-say-rah ah-vay-nee-dah.
They live on Third Avenue.

España es uno de los países más bellos de Europa.
ays-pah'nya ays oo'noh day lohs pah-ee'says
mahs bay'yohs day ayoo-roh'pah.
Spain is one of the most beautiful countries in Europe.

La Habana es la capital de Cuba.
lah ah-bah'nah ays lah kah-pee-tahl' day koo'bah.
Havana is the capital of Cuba.

Ella tiene el pelo rubio y los ojos azules.
ay'yah teeay'nay ayl pay'loh roo'bee-oh ee lòhs oh'hohs ah-soo'lays.
She has blonde hair and blue eyes.

Siempre tiene las manos en los bolsillos.
seeaym'pray teeay'nay lahs mah'nohs ayn lohs bohl-see'yohs.
He always keeps his hands in his pockets.

El manejar (conducir) cuidadosamente evita los accidentes.
ayl mah-nay-hahr' (kohn-doo-seer') kwee-dah-doh-sah-mayn'tay
ay-vee'tah lohs ahk-see-dayn'tays.
Careful driving promotes traffic safety.

Cuesta cincuenta centavos la libra.
kooay'stah seen-kooayn'tah sayn-tah'vohs lah lee'brah.
It costs 50 cents a pound.

El es dependiente.	**Ella es bailarina.**
ayl ays day-payn-deeayn'tay.	*ay'yah ays bahee-lah-ree'nah.*
He is a clerk.	She is a dancer.
¡Qué tonto!	**¡Qué lástima! (¡Qué pena!)**
kay' tohn'toh!	*kay lahs'tee-mah! (kay pay'nah)!*
What a fool!	What a pity!

SENTENCES USING *ANYBODY* AND *ANYTHING*
(Indefinite Pronouns; See 4.6; 1.7; 10.5)

¿Ha venido alguien? Nadie ha llegado. Nadie ha venido.
ah vay-nee'doh ahl'geeayn. nah'deeay ah yay-gah'doh.
nah'deeay ah vay-nee'doh.
Has anybody come? No one has arrived. Nobody has come.

¿Ha estado alguien aquí? Alguien ha estado aquí.
ah ays-tah'doh ahl'geeayn ah-kee'? ahl'geeayn ah ays-tah'doh ah-kee'.
Has anybody been here? Somebody has been here.

¿Ha recibido usted cartas? Sí, recibí algunas.
   No, no he recibido ninguna.
ah ray-see-bee'doh oos-tayd' kahr'tahs? see', ray-see-bee' ahl-goo'nahs.
   noh, noh ay ray-see-bee'doh neen-goo'nah.
Have you received any letters? Yes, I received some.
   No, I have not received any.

¿Tiene usted revistas americanas? Sí, tengo algunas. Allí hay una.
teeay'nay oos-tayd' ray-vees'tahs ah-may-ree-kah'nahs?
   see' tayn'goh ahl-goo'nahs. ah-yee' ahee oo'nah.
Have you got any American magazines? Yes, I have some.
   There is one.

¿Tiene usted periódicos ingleses? Lo siento. No tengo ninguno.
teeay-nay oos-tayd' pay-reeoh'dee-kohs een-glay'says?
   loh seeayn'toh. noh tayn'goh neen-goo'noh.
Have you got any English newspapers? I'm sorry. I don't have any.

¿Tiene usted fósforos? Lo siento. No.
teeay'nay oos-tayd' fohs'foh-rohs (oon fohs'foh-roh)?
   loh seeayn'toh. noh.
Have you got a match? Sorry. No.

¿Venden leche aquí? Sí, la vendemos. Por favor, déme una botella.
vayn'dayn lay'chay ah-kee'? see', lah vayn-day'mohs.
   pohr fah-vohr', day'may oo'nah boh-tay'yah.
Do you sell milk here? Yes, we do. Please give me a bottle.

¿Tiene usted dinero? No, no tengo dinero.
teeay'nay oos-tayd' dee-nay'roh? noh, noh tayn'goh dee-nay'roh
Have you got any money? No, I have no money.

¿Qué comió usted? Comí queso.
kay koh-meeoh' oos-tayd'? koh-mee' kay'soh.
What did you eat? I ate some cheese.

¿Qué compró usted? Compré algunos vestidos y un traje.
kay kohm-proh' oos-tayd'? kohm-pray' ahl-goo'nohs
   vays-tee'dohs ee oon trah'hay.
What did you buy? I bought some dresses and a suit.

¿Qué mira usted? Estoy mirando algunos discos interesantes.
kay mee'rah oos-tayd'. ays-tohee' mee-rahn'doh
   ahl-goo'nohs dees'kohs een-tay-ray-sahn'-tays.
What are you looking at? I am looking at some interesting records.

SENTENCES ON ADJECTIVES
(See 3.1-6, especially 3.6)

Elena es más alta que María.
ay-lay'nah ays mahs' ahl'tah kay mah-ree'ah.
Helen is taller than Mary.

Alicia es menos graciosa que Isabelita.
ah-lee'seeah ays may-nohs grah-seeoh'sah kay ee-sah-bay-lee'tah.
Alice is less witty than Betty.

Catalina es tan alta como María.
kah-tah-lee'nah ays tahn ahl'tah koh'moh mah-ree'ah.
Kate is as tall as Mary.

Catalina no es tan alta como Ana.
kah-tah-lee'nah noh ays tahn ahl'tah koh'moh ah'nah.
Kate is not so tall as Ann.

Ana es la más alta de las muchachas.
ah'nah ays lah mahs ahl'tah day lahs moo-chah'chahs.
Ann is the tallest of the girls.

Esta calle tiene más tránsito.
ays'tah kah'yay teeay'nay mahs trahn'see-toh.
This street has more traffic.

Tomaré un poco más de carne.
toh-mah-ray' oon poh'koh mahs day kahrr'nay.
I will take a little more meat.

Por favor, tome más.   **No deseo más.**
pohr fah-vohrr' toh'may mahs.   *noh day-say'oh mahs.*
Please have some more.   I don't want any more.

No quieren permanecer más aquí.
noh keeay'rayn payr-mahnay-sayr' mahs ah-kee'.
They don't want to stay here any longer.

Ya no puede ir allá.
yah noh pooay'day eerr ah-yah'.
He can no longer go there.

La muchacha vestida de seda azul fué elegida reina del baile. (See 3.4)
lah moo-chah'chah vays-tee'dah day say'dah ah-sool' fooay'
   ay-lay-hee'dah rayee'nah dayl bahee'lay.
The girl with the blue silk dress was elected the queen of the ball.

Mi amigo, el alto, tiene un automóvil nuevo.
mee ah-mee'goh ayl ahl'toh teeay'nay oon
ahoo-toh-moh'veel nooay'voh.
My tall friend owns a new car.

La bella muchacha española no vino a vernos.
lah bay'yah moo-chah'chah ays-pah-nyoh'lah
noh vee'noh ah vayrr-nohs.
The beautiful Spanish girl didn't come to see us.

THE BASIC TYPES OF SENTENCES
(See 10.6, 10.7)

Affirmative:	**Esta lección es fácil.** *ays'tah layk-seeohn' ays fah'seel.* This lesson is easy.
Negative:	**Esta lección no es difícil.** *ays'tah lyak-seeohn' noh ays dee-fee'seel.* This lesson is not difficult.

¿Es fácil esta lección?   **Es fácil.**
ays fah'seel ays'tah layk-seeohn'?   *ays fah'seel.*
Interrogative: Is this lesson easy?   It's easy.

¿No es grande este cuarto?   **Sí, es grande.**
noh ays grahn'day ays'tay kwahrr'toh?   *see, ays grahn'day.*
Isn't this room large?   Yes, it's large.

Le di el libro a María. (See 2.4)   **Se lo di a María.**
lay dee' ayl lee'broh ah mah-ree'ah.   *say loh dee ah mah-ree'ah.*
I gave Mary the book.   I gave it to Mary.

Se lo di a él.   **Ella fué allí.**
say loh dee ah ayl.   *ay'yah fooay' ah-yee'.*
I gave it to him.   She went there.

¿No fueron ellos allí?   **Sí, fueron.**
noh fooay'rohn ay-yohs ah-yee'?   *see, fooay'rohn.*
Didn't they go there?   Yes, they did.

Quiero ir a la escuela.
keeay'roh eerr ah lah ays-kway'lah.
I want to go to school.

Usted no quiere ir a la escuela.
oos-tayd' noh keeay'ray eerr ah lah ays-kway'lah.
You don't want to go to school.

¿De veras quieren ir a la escuela?
day vay'rahs keeay'rayn eerr ah lah ays-kway'lah?
Do they really want to go to school?

**Los que estudian idiomas con discos pueden pronunciar correctamente
        y aprender más fácilmente. (See 4.7; 7.1-3)**
*lohs kay ays-too' deeahn ee-deeoh'mahs kohn dees'kohs pooay'dayn
        proh-noon-seeahrr' coh-rrayk-tah-mayn'tay ee ah-prayn-dayrr'
        mahs fah-seel-mayn'tay.*
Those who study languages with records can pronounce them cor-
        rectly and learn them easily.

¿Quién es la dama con quien lo vi a usted anoche?
*keeayn' ays lah dah'mah kohn keeayn'
        loh vee ah oos-tayd' ah-noh'chay?*
Who is the lady with whom I saw you last night?

Es mi tía que acaba de llegar de Europa.
ays mee tee'ah kay ah-kah'bah day yay-gahr' day ayoo-roh'pah.
She is my aunt who just came from Europe.

La muchacha con quien yo hablaba es mi novia.
lah moo-chah'chah kohn keeayn yoh ah-blah'bah ays mee noh-veeah.
The girl to whom I was speaking is my fiancée.

El muchacho cuyo padre es mi maestro, vive aquí.
*ayl moo-chah'choh koo'yoh pah'dray ays mee mah-ays'troh
        vee'vay ah-kee'.*
The boy whose father is my teacher lives here.

Cuando ella vino, él se fué.
kwahn'doh ay'yah vee'noh ayl say fooay'.
When she came, he left.

Si Juan viene, se lo diré.
see hooahn veeay'nay say loh dee-ray'.
If John comes, I will tell him about it.

Si Juan hubiera (hubiese) venido se lo habría dicho. (See 10.3)
*see hooahn oo-beeay'rah (oo-beeay'say) vay-nee'doh say loh ah-bree'ah
        dee'choh.*
If John had come, I would have told him about.

Cuando venga Juan se lo diré.
kwahn'doh vayn'gah hooahn say loh dee-ray'.
When John comes, I will tell him about it.

EVERYDAY CONVERSATIONS

BASIC EXPRESSIONS

Buenos días.
bway'nohs dee'ahs.
Good morning.

Buenas tardes.
bway'nahs tahr'days.
Good afternoon.

Buenas noches.
bway'nahs noh'chays.
Good evening. Good night.

¿Qué tal?
kay' tahl?
Hello.

Adiós.
ah-dee-ohs'.
Goodbye.

Muchas gracias.
moo'chas grah'see-ahs.
Thank you.

De nada.
day nah'dah.
You're welcome.

Perdóneme.
payr-doh'nay-may.
Excuse me.

Por favor.
pohr fah-vohrr'.
Please.

Hable más despacio.
ah'blay mahs days-pah'see-oh.
Speak more slowly.

¿Cuánto?
kwahn'toh?
How much?

¿Dónde?
dohn'day?
Where?

¿Cuándo?
kwahn'doh.
When?

Déme.
day'may.
Give me.

¿Dónde está (están)?
dohn'day ays-tah' (ays-tahn')?
Where is (are)?

Me llamo Ramón.
may yah-moh rah-mohn'.
My name is Ramon.

¿Habla usted inglés?
ah'blah oos-tayd' een-glays'?
Do you speak English?

No entiendo.
noh ayn-tee-ayn'doh.
I don't understand.

¿Cómo le va?
koh'moh lay vah?
How do you do?

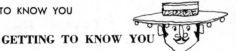

GETTING TO KNOW YOU

Tengo el gusto de presentarle al Señor López.
*tayn'goh ayl goos'toh day pray-sayn-tahr'lay ahl
        say-nyohrr' loh'pays.*
May I present Mr. Lopez.

Encantado de conocerlo.   **Mi esposa.**
ayn-kahn-tah'doh day koh-noh-sayr'loh.   *mee ays-poh'sah.*
Very pleased to meet you.   My wife.

Y éste es mi hijo (hija).
ee ays'tay ays mee ee'hoh (ee'hah).
And this is my son (daughter).

¿Cómo esta usted?   **Muy bien, gracias.**
koh'moh ays-tah' oos-tayd'?   *moo'ee bee-ayn', grah'see-ahs.*
How do you do?   Very well, thank you.

Tiene una casa muy acogedora.
tee-ay'nay oo'nah kah'sah moo'ee ah-koh-hay-doh'rah.
You have a charming house.

¡Qué preciosa vista tiene desde esta ventana!
*kay pray-see-oh'sah vees'tah teeay'-nay days'day ays'tah
        vayn-tah'nah!*
What a lovely view you have from this window!

¡Qué cuarto tan bonito!
kay kwahr'toh tahn boh-nee'toh!
Isn't this a beautiful room!

¿Ha estado mucho tiempo en el país?
ah ays-tah'doh moo'choh tee-aym'poh ayn ayl pah-ees'?
Have you been in the country very long?

Solamente diez días.
soh-lah-mayn'tay deeays' dee'ahs.
Only 10 days.

¿Cuánto tiempo piensa quedarse?
kwahn'toh tee-aym'poh pee-ayn'sah kay-dahr'say?
How long are you planning to stay?

Regresaremos en cinco días.
ray-gray-sah-ray'mohs ayn seen'koh dee'ahs.
We shall return in 5 days.

Espero que su estada sea agradable.
ays-pay'roh kay soo ays-tah'dah say-ah ah-grah-dah'blay.
I hope you have a pleasant stay.

¿Le gusta México?	**Es un país precioso.**
lay goos'tah may'hee-koh?	*ays oon pah-ees' pray-see-oh'soh.*
Do you like Mexico?	It is a beautiful country.

Espero que tenga un feliz regreso.
ays-pay'roh kay tayn'gah oon fay-lees' ray-gray'soh.
I hope you have a good trip home.

¿En qué parte de los Estados Unidos vive usted?
*ayn kay pahr'tay day lohs ays-tah'dohs oo-nee'dohs vee'vay
oos-tayd'?*
Where do you live in the United States?

Vivo en Boston.	**¿Está aquí en viaje de negocios?**
vee'voh ayn bohs'tohn.	*ays-tah'ah-kee' ayn vee-ah'hay day nay-goh'*
I live in Boston.	Are you here on a business trip? [*see-ohs?*

No, soy turista.
Noh, soh'ee too-rees'tah.
No, I am a tourist.

¿Cuántos hijos tiene usted?
kwahn'tohs ee'hohs tee-ay'nay oos-tayd'?
How many children do you have?

He pasado una tarde muy agradable.
ay pah-sah'doh oo'nah tahr'day moo'ee ah-grah-dah'blay.
I have had a very pleasant evening.

Nos divertimos muchísimo.
nohs dee-vayr-tee'mohs moo-chee'see-moh.
We enjoyed ourselves very much.

Muchísimas gracias por sus gentilezas.
*moo-chee'see-mahs grah'see-ahs pohr soos hayn-tee-lay'sahs.
ah-tayn-see-oh'nays.*
Thank you very much for your hospitality.

COUNTING

The Cardinal Numbers

uno
oo'noh
one

dos
dohs
two

tres
trays
three

cuatro
kwah'troh
four

cinco
seen'koh
five

seis
sayees
six

siete
see-ay'tay
seven

ocho
oh'choh
eight

nueve
nway'vay
nine

diez
dee-ays'
ten

once
ohn'say
eleven

doce
doh'say
twelve

trece
tray'say
thirteen

catorce
kah-tohr'say
fourteen

quince
keen'say
fifteen

dieciseis
dee-ays-ee-says'
sixteen

diecisiete
dee-ays-ee-see-ay'tay
seventeen

dieciocho
dee-ays-ee-oh'-choh
eighteen

diecinueve
dee-ays-ee-nway'vay
nineteen

veinte
vayn-tay
twenty

veintiuno
vayn-tee-oo'noh
twenty-one

treinta
trayn'tah
thirty

cuarenta
kwah-rayn'tah
forty

cincuenta
seen-kwayn'tah
fifty

sesenta
say-sayn'tah
sixty

setenta
say-tayn'tah
seventy

ochenta
oh-chayn'tah
eighty

noventa
noh-vayn'tah
ninety

cien
see-ayn'
one hundred

doscientos
dohs-see-ayn'tohs
two hundred

The Ordinal Numbers

primero
pree-may'roh
first

quinto
kween'toh
fifth

noveno
noh-vay'noh
ninth

segundo
say-goon'doh
second

sexto
say'stoh
sixth

décimo
day'see-moh
tenth

tercero
tayr-say'roh
third

séptimo
sayp'tee-moh
seventh

undécimo
oon-day'see-moh
eleventh

cuarto
kwahr'toh
fourth

octavo
ohk-tah'-voh
eighth

duodécimo
doo-oh-day'see-moh
twelfth

The Fractions

medio
may'deeoh
half

un cuarto
oon kwahr'toh
one fourth

un octavo
oon ohk-tah'voh
one eighth

un tercio
oon tayr'seeoh
a third

tres cuartos
trays kwahr'tohs
three quarters

un doceavo
oon doh-say-ah'voh
one twelfth

THE CLOCK AND THE CALENDAR

¿Qué hora es?
kay oh'rah ays?
What time is it?

Son las diez (de la mañana)
sohn lahs deeays (day lah mah-nyah'nah).
It is ten a.m.

Son las tres y cuarto (de la tarde).
sohn lahs trays ee kwahr'toh (day lah tahr'day).
It is a quarter past three p.m.

Son las siete y media.
sohn lahs seeay'tay ee may'deeah.
It is half past seven.

Son las nueve menos cuarto.
sohn lahs nooay'vay may'nohs kwahr'toh.
It is quarter to nine.

Los días de la semana son: lunes, martes, miércoles, jueves, viernes, sábado, domingo.

lohs dee'ahs day lah say-mah'nah sohn: loo'nays, mahr'tays, meeayr'-koh-lays, hway-vays, veeayr'nays, sah'bah-doh, doh-meen'goh.

The days of the week are: Monday, Tuesday, Wednesday, Thursday, Friday, Saturday, Sunday.

Los meses del año son: enero, febrero, marzo, abril, mayo, junio, julio, agosto, septiembre, octubre, noviembre, diciembre.

lohs may'says dayl ah'nyoh sohn: ay-nay'roh, fay-bray'roh, mahr'soh, ah-breel', mah'yoh, hoo'neeoh, hoo'leeoh, ah-gohs'toh, sayp-teeaym'bray, ohk-too'bray, noh-veeaym'bray, dee-seeaym'bray.

The months of the year are: January, February, March, April, May, June, July, August, September, October, November, December.

Las estaciones del año son: primavera, verano, otoño, invierno.

lahs ays-tah-seeoh'nays dayl ah'nyoh sohn: pree-mah-vay'rah, vay-rah'noh, oh-toh'nyoh, een-veeayr'noh.

The seasons of the year are: Spring, Summer, Autumn, Winter.

Los días de fiesta más importantes son: Año Nuevo, Pascua (Florida, Pascua de Resurrección) y Navidades (Pascuas).

lohs dee'ahs day feeays'tah mahs eem-pohr-tahn'tays sohn: ah'nyoh nooay-voh, pahs'kooah (floh-ree'dah, pahs'kooah day ray-soo-rrayk-seeohn') ee nah-vee-dah'days (pahs'kooahs).

The most important holidays are: New Year's Day, Easter and Christmas.

Cumplo treinta años el diecisiete de julio de mil novecientos sesenta y siete.

koom'ploh tray'een-tah ah'nyohs ayl deeay-see-seeay'tay day hoo'leeoh day meel noh-vay-seeayn'tohs say-sayn'tah ee seeay'tay.

I'll be thirty years old on July 17, 1967.

¿Qué tiempo hace? (¿Cómo está el tiempo?)

kay teeaym'poh ah'say? (koh-moh ays-tah' ayl teeaym'poh)?

How is the weather?

Hace buen tiempo.   **Hace un bonito día.**

ah'say booayn teeaym'poh.   *ah'say oon boh-nee'toh dee'ah.*

It is fine.   It is a beautiful day.

Está lloviendo (nevando).

ays-tah' yoh-veeayn'doh (nay-vahn'doh).

It is raining (snowing).

Cae un aguacero. (Está lloviznando).
kah'ay oon ah-gooah-say'roh. (ays-tah' yoh-vees-nahn'doh).
It is showering (drizzling).

STRANGER IN TOWN

¿Hay alguien aquí que hable inglés?
ahee ahl'geeayn ah-kee' kay ah'blay een-glays'?
Is there anyone here who speaks English?

Me he perdido.
may ay payr-dee'doh.
I've lost my way.

¿A dónde quiere usted ir?
ah dohn'day keeay'ray oos-tayd' eerr?
Where do you want to go?

¿Me entiende usted?
may ayn-teeayn'day oos-tayd'?
Do you understand me?

No, no entiendo.
Noh, noh ayn-teeayn'doh.
No, I don't understand.

Por favor, hable despacio.
pohr fah-vohrr', ah'blay days-pah'seeoh.
Please speak slowly.

Por favor, repita.
pohr fah-vohrr', ray-pee' tah.
Please repeat.

¿Qué dice usted?
kay dee'say oos-tayd'?
What are you saying?

No puedo hallar mi billetera.
noh pooay'doh ah-yahr' mee bee-yay-tay'rah.
I can't find my wallet.

¡Me han robado!
may ahn roh-bah'doh!
I've been robbed!

¡Policía!
poh-lee-see'ah!
Police!

¡Llame a la policía!
yah'may ah lah poh-lee-see'ah!
Call the police!

¿(En) dónde está la estación de policía?
(ayn) dohn'day ays-tah' lah ays-tah-seeohn' day poh-lee-see'ah?
Where is the Police Station?

Por allí.
pohr ah-yee'.
That way.

¡Auxilio! ¡(Socorro!)
ahoo-gsee'leeoh! (soh-koh'rroh!)
Help!

¡Fuego!
fooay'goh!
Fire!

Soy norteamericano
sohee nohr-tay-ah-may-ree-kah'noh.
I am an American.

Lléveme al consulado americano.
yay-vay-may ahl kohn-soo-lah'doh ah-may-ree-kah'noh.
Take me to the American consulate.

He dejado mi abrigo en el tren.
ay day-hah'doh mee ah-bree'goh ayn ayl trrayn.
I've left my overcoat on the train.

¿Cómo puedo recuperarlo?
koh'moh pooay'doh rray-koo-pay-rahr'loh?
How can I get it back?

No puedo hallar mi hotel.
noh pooay'doh ah-yahrr' mee oh-tayl'.
I cannot find my hotel.

¿Puede usted ayudarme?
pooay'day oos-tayd' ah-yoo-dahr'may?
Can you help me?

He perdido mi paraguas.
ay payr-dee'doh mee pah-rah'gooahs.
I've lost my umbrella.

¿Puede usted decirme dónde está la oficina de objetos perdidos?
*pooay-day oos-tayd' day-seer'may dohn'day ays-tah' lah oh-fee-see'nah
day ohb-hay'tohs payr-dee'dohs?*
Can you tell me where the lost and found desk is?

He perdido una maleta.   **Lleva las iniciales R. G. F.**
ay payr-dee'doh oo'nah mah-lay'tah.   *yah'vah lahsee-nee-seeah'lays*
I have lost a suitcase.   *ay'ray hay ay'fay.*
It carries the initials R. G. F.

¿Tiene usted alguna que corresponda a esa descripción?
*teeay'ne oos-tayd' ahl-goo'nah kay koh-rrays-pohn'dah ah ay'sah
days-kreep-seeohn'?*
Have you a piece answering that description?

Si llega, llámeme al teléfono 11-05-55.
see yah'gah, yah'may-may ahl tay-lay'foh-noh ohn'say-say'roh seen'koh.
If it comes in, telephone me at 11-05-55.   *seen-kwayn'tah ee seen'koh.*

(In Emergencies)

Está preso.
ays-tah' pray'soh.
You are under arrest.

¿A dónde me lleva?
ah dohn'day may yay-vah?
Where are you taking me?

A la delegación.
ah lah day-lay-gah-see-ohn'.
To the police station.

Necesito un abogado.
nay-say-see'toh oon ah-boh-gah'doh.
I need a lawyer.

Deseo hablar por teléfono.
day-say'oh ah-blahr' pohr tay-lay' foh-noh.
I would like to use the phone.

¿Está herido?
ays-tah' ay-ree'doh?
Are you hurt?

Debemos llamar a un policía.
day-bay'mohs yah-mahr' ah oon poh-lee-see'ah.
We should send for a policeman.

Por favor, déme su nombre y dirección.
pohr fah-vohrr', day'may soo nohm'bray ee dee-rayk-see-ohn'.
Please let me have your name and address.

Permítame ver su licencia de manejar.
payr-mee'tah-may vayr soo lee-sayn'see-ah day mah-nay-hahr'.
Let me see your driver's license.

¿Cómo se llama su compañía de seguro?
koh'moh say yah'mah soo kohm-pah-nyee'ah day say-goo'roh?
What is the name of your insurance company?

¿Tiene averías su coche?
tee-ay'nay ah-vay-ree'ahs soo koh'chay?
How badly damaged is your car?

He perdido mi tarjeta de turista.
ay payr-dee'doh mee tahr-hay'tah day too-rees'tan.
I have lost my tourist card.

¿Puedo reponerla?
poo-ay'doh ray-poh-nayr'lah?
Can I get a replacement?

¿Cuánto cobran?
kwahn'toh koh'brahn?
What is the charge?

ABOARD SHIP

Viajo en segunda clase. Camarote número veinticuatro.
veeah'hoh ayn say-goon'dah klah'say. kah-mah-roh'tay
noo'may-roh vayeen-tee-kooah'troh.
I am traveling cabin class. Stateroom No. 24.

¿Puede usted indicarme dónde está?
pooay'day oos-tayd' een-dee-kahr'may dohn'day ays-tah'?
Can you please direct me?

Usted está en la cubierta C.
oos-tayd' ays-tah' ayn lah koo-beeayrr'tah say.
You are on C deck.

Lleve nuestras maletas a nuestro camarote.
yay'vay nooays'trahs mah-lay'tahs ah nooays'troh kah-mah-roh'tay.
Take our bags to our cabin.

¿Puedo tomar el ascensor para ir a mi camarote?
pooay'doh toh-mahrr' ayl ahs-sayn-sohrr' pah'rah eerr ah mee
kah-mah-roh'tay?
Can I take the elevator to my cabin?

¿En qué dirección está?
ayn kay dee-rayk-seeohn' ays-tah'?
In what direction is it?

¿A qué hora se sirve el almuerzo?
ah kay oh'rah say seerr'vay ayl ahl-mooayr'soh?
What time is lunch served?

El primer turno es a las doce.
ayl pree-mayr' toorr'noh ays ah lahs doh'say.
The first sitting is at twelve.

El segundo a la una.
ayl say-goon'doh ah lah oo'nah.
The second at one.

¿A qué hora se sirve la cena?
ah kay oh'rah say seerr'vay lah say'nah?
At what time is dinner served?

La cena se sirve a las seis.
lah say'nah say seerr'vay ah lahs sayees.
Dinner is served at six.

Quisiera alquilar una silla de cubierta.
kee-seeay'rah ahl-kee-lahrr' oo'nah see'yah day koo-beeayr'tah.
I would like to rent a deck chair.

¿Cuánto cuesta una silla de cubierta?
kwahn'toh kooays'tah oo'nah see'yah day koo-beeayr'tah?
How much does a deck chair cost?

Cuesta dos dólares (pesos).
kways'tah dohs doh'lah-rays (pays'sohs).
The cost is 2 dollars.

¿A qué hora atraca el barco mañana?
ah kay oh'rah ah-trrah'kah ayl bahr'koh mah-nyah'nah?
At what time does the boat dock tomorrow?

Atracaremos a las ocho.
ah-trrah-kah-ray'mohs ah lahs oh'choh.
We will dock at 8:00.

Ocúpese de sacar mi equipaje a tiempo.
oh-koo'pay-say day sah-kahrr' mee ay-kee-pah'hay ah teeaym'poh.
See that my baggage is off in time.

PLANE TRAVEL

¿Hay un avión para Caracas?
ah-ee oon ah-vee-ohn' pah'rah kah-rah'kahs?
Is there a plane for Caracas?

¿A qué hora sale?
ah kay oh'rah sah'lay?
What time does it leave?

¿Cuánto dura el vuelo?
kwan'toh doo' rah ayl voo-ay'loh?
How long is the flight?

¿Cuánto cuesta el viaje?
kwahn'toh kways'tah ayl vee-ah'hay?
How much is the fare?

Un boleto para Buenos Aires, por favor.
oon boh-lay'toh pah'rah booay'nohs ah'ee-rays, pohr fah-vohrr'.
A ticket to Buenos Aires, please.

Deseo comprar un boleto para el próximo vuelo.
day-say'oh kohm-prahr' oon boh-lay'toh pah'rah ayl prohk'see-moh
I'd like to buy a seat on the next flight. [*vway'loh.*

Un asiento cerca de la ventana, por favor.
oon ah-see-ayn'toh sayr'kah day lah vayn-tah'nah, pohr fah-vohrr'.
A seat next to the window, please.

¿A qué hora sale el autobús para el aeropuerto?
ah kay oh'rah sah'lay ayl ahoo-toh-boos' pah-rah ayl ah-ay-roh-pooayr'toh?
When does the bus leave for the airport?

¿Se sirve comida (cena) en este viaje?
say seer'vay koh-mee'dah (say-nah) ayn ays'tay vee-ah'hay?
Is lunch (dinner) served on this flight?

¿Cuánto pesa mi equipaje?
kwahn'toh pay'sah mee ay-kee-pah'hay?
How much does my baggage weigh?

Tiene cinco libras de exceso de equipaje.
tee-ay'nay seen-koh lee'brahs day ayk-say'soh day ay-kee-pah'hay.
You are five pounds overweight.

Empacaré otra vez.
aym-pah-kah-ray' oh'trah vays.
I will repack my luggage.

¿Cuánto cuesta por libra?
kwahn'toh kways'tah pohr lee'brah?
What is the charge per pound?

Se cobra doce pesos por kilo.
say koh'brah doh'say pay'sohs pohr kee'loh.
The rate is 12 dollars per kilo.

Pagaré el exceso de equipaje.
pah-gah-ray' ayl ayk-say'soh day ay-kee-pah'hay.
I will pay for the overweight.

¿Dónde está el avión para San Salvador?
dohn'day ays-tah' ayl ah-vee-ohn' pah'rah sahn sahl-vah-dohr'?
Where is the plane for San Salvador?

Allá, señor.
ah-yah' say-nyorr'.
Over there, sir.

Su boleto, por favor.
soo boh-lay'toh pohr fah-vohrr'.
May I see your ticket, please.

Tiene el asiento número 8B.
tee-ay'nay ayl ah-see ayn'toh noo'may-roh oh'choh bay.
You have seat number 8B.

Amárrense sus cinturones de seguridad.
ah-mah'rrayn-say soos seen-too-roh'nays day
        say-goo-ree-dahd'.
Fasten your safety belts.

¿Señorita, llegará a tiempo el avión?
say-nyo-ree'tah yay-gah-rah' ah tee-aym'poh ayl ah-vee-ohn'?
Stewardess, will the plane land on schedule?

¿Me permite un chicle, por favor?
may payr-mee'tay oon chee'klay, pohr fah-vohrr'?
May I have some chewing-gum, please?

Señorita, me siento mareado.
say-nyoh-ree'tah, may see-ayn'toh mah-ree-ah'doh.
Stewardess, I feel airsick.

¿Tiene usted algún remedio?
tee-ay'nay ahl-goon'ray-may'dee-oh?
Do you have a remedy?

ALL ABOARD

Un boleto para Lima.
oon boh-lay'toh pah-rah lee'mah.
One ticket to Lima.

¿Cuánto cuesta el boleto?
kwahn'toh kways'tah ayl boh-lay'toh?
How much is the ticket?

Primera clase.
pree-may'rah klah'say.
First class.

Segunda clase.
say-goon'dah klah'say.
Second class.

Viaje sencillo.
vee-ah'hay sayn-see'yoh.
One way.

Ida y vuelta.
ee-dah ee vooayl'tah.
Round trip.

¿A qué hora sale este tren?
ah kay oh'rah sah'lay ays'tay trayn?
What time does this train leave?

¿A qué hora llega?
ah kay oh'rah yay'gah?
When does it arrive?

¿Es expreso o local?
ays ayks-pray'-soh oh loh-kahl'?
Is it an express or a local?

¿Está tomado este asiento?
ays-tah' toh-mah'doh ays'tay ah-see-ayn'toh?
Is this seat taken?

Boletos, por favor.
boh-lay'tohs pohr fah-vohrr'.
Tickets, please.

¿Se permite fumar aquí?
say payr-mee'tay foo-mahr' ah-kee'?
Is smoking permitted here?

El carro comedor está abierto.
ayl kah'rroh koh-may-dohrr' ays-tah' ah-bee-ayr'toh.
The dining car is now open.

¿Dónde está el baño por favor?
dohn'day ays-tah' ayl bah-nyoh' pohr fah-vohrr'?
Which way to the lavatory, please?

¿Llega a tiempo el tren?
yay'gah ah tee-aym'poh ayl trayn?
Is the train on time?

Sí, llegaremos en diez minutos.
see', yay-gah-ray'mohs ayn deeays mee-noo-tohs.
Yes, we arrive in 10 minutes.

GOING THROUGH CUSTOMS

Abran sus maletas.
ah'brahn soos mah-lay'tahs.
Open your bags.

¿Cuántos cigarrillos trae?
kwahn'tohs see-gah-rree'yohs trah'ay?
How many cigarettes are you bringing in?

¿Trae algo que no sea objeto de uso personal?
trah ay ahl'goh kay noh say-ah ohb-hay'toh day oo'soh payr-soh-nahl'?
Do you have anything besides personal effects?

¿Dónde se hizo esto?
dohn'day say ee'soh ays'toh?
Where was this made?

¿Cuántos rollos de película tiene?
kwahn'tohs roh'yohs day pay-lee'koo-lah tee-ay'nay?
How many rolls of film do you have?

¿Dónde está su documentación, por favor?
dohn'day ays-tah' soo doh-koo-mayn-tah-see-ohn', pohr fah-vohrr'?
Where are your papers, please?

Su tarjeta de turista.
soo tahr-hay'tah day too-rees'tah.
Your tourist card.

¿Cuánto tiempo piensa quedarse?
kwahn'toh tee-aym'poh pee-ayn'sah kay-dahr'say?
How long do you intend to stay?

Espero que le vaya bien aquí con nosotros.
*ays-pay'roh kay lay vah'yah bee-ayn' ah-kee' kohn
        noh-soh'trohs.*
I hope you have a nice stay with us.

¿Quiere conseguirme un maletero, por favor?
kee-ay'ray kohn-say-geer'may oon mah-lay-tay'roh pohr fah-vohrr'?
Will you please get a porter for me?

Maletero, por favor lleve mis maletas.
mah-lay-tay'roh, por fah-vohrr' yay'-vay mees mah-lay'tahs.
Porter, please take my bags.

Al sitio de taxis.
ahl see'tee-oh day tahk'sees.
To the taxi stand.

A la estación de autobuses.
ah lah ays-tah-see-ohn' day ahoo-toh-boo'says.
To the bus station.

¿Cuánto cobra?
kwahn'toh koh'brah?
How much do you charge?

Eso es demasiado.
ay'soh ays day-mah-see-ah'doh.
That is too high.

Le pagaré diez pesos (centavos).
lay pah-gah-ray' deeays pay'sohs (sayn-tah'vohs).
I will pay you 10 pesos (centavos).

TAXI!

¡Taxi!
tah'gsee!
Taxi!

Lléveme al distrito comercial.
yay-vay-may ahl dees-tree'toh koh-mayrr-seeahl'.
Take me to the shopping center.

Tengo prisa.
tayn'goh pree'sah.
I'm in a hurry.

Pare en la esquina.
pah'ray ayn lah ays-kee'nah.
Stop at the corner.

¿Qué edificio es ése a la derecha (a la izquierda)?
kay ay-dee-fee'seeoh ays ay'say ah lah day-ray'chah (ah lah ees-keeayr'dah)?
What's this building on the right (on the left)?

¿Cuánto es?
kwahn'toh ays?
What's the charge?

BUS STOP

¿Dónde se toma el autobús para Acapulco?
dohn'day say toh'mah ayl ahoo-toh-boos' pah'rah ah-kah-pool'koh?
Where do I get the bus for Acapulco?

¿A qué hora sale el próximo autobús?
ah kay oh'rah sah'lay ayl prohg'zee-moh ahoo-toh-boos'?
What time does the next bus leave?

¿Cuánto cuesta el pasaje?
kwahn'toh kways'tah ayl pah-sah'hay?
What is the fare?

¿Puedo reservar un asiento?
pway'doh ray-sayr-vahr' oon ah-see-ayn'toh?
Can I reserve a seat?

¿Hace escalas este autobús?
ah'say ays-kah'lahs ays'tay ahoo-toh-boos'?
Is this a through bus?

Los boletos por favor.
lohs boh-lay'tohs pohr fah-vohrr'?
Tickets, please.

¿A qué pueblo llegaremos?
ah kay poo-ay'bloh yay-gah-ray' mohs?
What town are we coming to?

¿Qué estamos pasando a la derecha (izquierda)?
kay ays-tah'mohs pah-sahn'doh ah lah day-ray'cha (ees-kee-ayr'dah)?
What are we passing on the right (left)?

¿Cuándo llegamos a Cuernavaca?
kwahn'doh yay-gah'mohs ah kooayr-nah-vah'kah?
How soon do we arrive in Cuernavaca?

MOTORING THROUGH LATIN AMERICA

¿Cuido su coche, señor?
kwee'doh soo koh'chay, say-nyorr'?
Watch your car, sir?

Gire a la derecha.
hee'ray ah lah day-raychah.
Turn the wheel to the right.

Derecho hacia atrás.
day-ray'chah ah'see-ah ah-trahs'
Straight back.

Corte a la izquierda (derecha).
kohr'tay ah lah ees-kee-ayr'dah (day-ray'chah).
Cut sharply to the left (right).

¿Hay una estación de gasolina cerca?
Ah-ee oo'nah ays-tah-see-ohn' day gah-soh-lee'nah sayr'kah?
Is there a gas station nearby?

Déme diez litros de gasolina.
day'may deeays lee'trohs day gah-soh-lee'nah.
Give me 10 liters of gas.

Llene el tanque.
yay'nay ayl tahn'kay.
Fill the tank.

Gasolina de alta potencia. Regular.
gah-soh-lee'nah day ahl'tah poh-tayn'seeah. ray-goo lahr'.
High octane. Regular.

Por favor, revise mis llantas.
pohr fah-vohrr', ray-vee'say mees yahn'tahs.
Please check my tires.

¿Es éste el camino a Puebla?
ays ays'tay ayl kah-mee'noh ah pooay'blah?
Is this the road to Puebla?

Derecho a quince kilómetros.
day-ray'choh ah keen'say kee-loh'may-trohs.
Straight ahead 15 kilometers.

Dé vuelta a la izquierda (derecha) en el crucero.
day vooayl'tah ah lah ees-keeayr'dah (day-ray'chah) ayn ayl
Turn left (right) at the crossroad.   [*kroo-say'roh.*

Hay una desviación a seis kilómetros de aquí.
Ah-ee oo'nah days-vee-ah-see-ohn' ah sayees kee-loh'may-trohs
        day ah-kee'.
There is a detour 6 kilometers from here.

Se me reventó una llanta.
say may rray-vayn-toh' oo'nah yahn'tah.
I have a flat tire.

No funcionan las luces (los faros).
noh foon-see-oh'nahn lahs loo'says (lohs fah-rohs).
My lights (headlights) don't work.

¿Dónde hacen composturas?
dohn'day ah'sayn kohm-pohs-too' rahs?
Where can I have repairs made?

Por favor, mande a alguien que arregle mi coche.
pohr fah-vohrr', mahn'day ah ahl'ghee-ayn kay ah-rray'glay mee koh'chay.
Please send someone to repair my car.

¿Me permite tomar agua para mi coche?
may payr-mee'tay toh-mahr' ah'gwah pah'rah mee koh'chay?
May I have some water for my car?

¿Me puede llevar a la estación de gasolina?
may pway'day yay-vahr' ah lah ays-tah-see-ohn' day gah-soh-lee'nah?
Please give me a lift to the gas station.

AT THE HOTEL

Hice una reservación por carta (por teléfono).
ee'say oo'nah ray-sayr-vah-see-ohn' pohr kahr'tah (pohr tay-lay'foh-noh).
I made a reservation by letter (by phone).

Reservé un cuarto sencillo (doble).
ray-sayr-vay' oon kwahr'toh sayn-see'yoh (doh'blay).
I reserved a single (double) room.

Deseo un cuarto con (sin) baño.
day-say'oh oon kwahr'toh kohn (seen) ban'yo.
I want a room with (without) bath.

¿Tiene un cuarto con cama doble (camas gemelas)?
tee-ay'nay oon kwahr'toh kohn kah'mah doh'blay (kah'mahs hay-may'lahs)?
Do you have a room with a double bed (twin beds)?

Este cuarto es muy pequeño (grande).
ays'tay kwahr'toh ays moo'ee pay-kay'nyoh (grahn'day).
This room is too small (large).

¿Cuánto cuesta este cuarto?
kwahn'toh kways'tah ays'tay kwahr'toh?
What is the price of this room?

¿Cuánto tiempo piensa quedarse?
kwahn'toh teeaym'poh pee-ayn'sah kay-dahr'say?
How long are you planning to stay?

Pienso quedarme cuatro días.
pee-ayn'soh kay-dahr'may kooah'troh dee'ahs.
I am planning to stay 4 days.

El precio por un solo día es ochenta pesos.
ll pray'see-oh pohr oon soh'loh dee ah ays oh-chayn'tah pay'sohs.
The price for a single day is 80 pesos.

Por semana hay un precio especial de quinientos pesos.
*pohr say-mah'nah ah-ee oon pray'see-oh ays-pay-see-ahl' day
kee-neeayn'tohs pay'sohs.*
For a week we have a special rate of 500 pesos.

¿Tiene usted algo más barato?
ee-ay-nay oos-tayd' ahl'goh mahs bah-rah'toh?
Do you have something cheaper?

¿Incluye las comidas?
en-kloo'yay lahs koh-mee'dahs?
Are meals included?

¿Está incluido el desayuno en el precio?
*ys-tah' een-kloo-eeh'doh ayl day-sah-yoo'noh ayn ayl
pray'see-oh?*
Is breakfast included in the price?

Firme el registro, por favor.
eer-may ayl ray-hees'troh, pohr fah-vohrr'.
Will you register, please?

Hágame el favor de llamar a las ocho de la mañana.
*h'gah-may ayl fah-vohr' day yah-mahr' ah lahs oh'cho day lah
mahn-yah'nah?*
Please call me at 8 o'clock in the morning.

¿A qué hora se sirve el desayuno?
h kay oh'rah say seer'vay ayl day-sah-yoo'noh?
What time is breakfast served?

¿Dónde está el comedor?
dohn'day ays-tah' ayl koh-may-dohr'?
Where is the dining room?

Espero una visita.
ays-pay'-roh oon'ah vee-see'tah.
I am expecting a visitor.

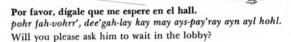

Por favor, dígale que me espere en el hall.
pohr fah-vohrr', dee'gah-lay kay may ays-pay'ray ayn ayl hohl.
Will you please ask him to wait in the lobby?

Desearía guardar unos valores en su caja fuerte.
*day-say-ah-ree'ah goo-ahr-dahr' oo'nohs vah-loh'rays ayn soo
        kah'hah foo-ayr'tah.*
I would like to check my valuables in your safe.

Por favor, permítame la llave de mi cuarto.
*pohr fah-vohrr', payr-mee' tah-may lah yah'vay day mee
        kwahr'toh.*
Please let me have the key to my room.

Pensamos irnos mañana.
payn-sah'mohs eer'nohs mahn-yah'nah.
We are planning to leave tomorrow.

Por favor, tenga lista nuestra cuenta.
pohr fah-vohrr' tayn'gah lees'tah noo-ays'trah kwayn'tah.
Please have our bill ready.

Por favor, mande a un muchacho por el equipaje.
*pohr fah-vohrr' mahn-day ah oon moo-cha'choh pohr ayl
        ay-kee-pah'hay.*
Please send a boy for our bags.

Tenga la amabilidad de llamar un taxi.
tayn'gah lah ah-mah-bee-lee-dahd' day yah-mahr' oon tak'see.
Kindly call a taxi.

Lo pasamos muy bien aquí.
loh pah-sah'mohs mooee beeayn ah-kee'.
We enjoyed our stay here very much.

RENTING A ROOM

¿Desea usted un cuarto amueblado o sin amueblar?
*day-say'ah oos-tayd' oon kwahrr'toh ah-mooay-blah'doh oh seen
ah-mooay-blahrr'?*
Do you want a furnished or unfurnished room?

Deseo un cuarto amueblado con baño.
day-say'oh oon kwahrr'toh ah-mooay-blah'doh kohn bah'nyoh.
I want a furnished room with bath.

¿Prefiere usted un cuarto con vista a la calle o al mar?
*pray-feeay'ray oos-tayd' oon kwahr'toh kohn vees'tah ah lah kah'yay
oh ahl mahr?*
Would you prefer a room which looks out on the street or on the sea?

Tomaré el de vista al mar.
toh-mah-ray' ayl day vees'tah ahl mahr.
I shall take the one with the view of the sea.

¿Cuánto cobrará usted, incluyendo impuestos y servicio?
*kwahn'toh koh-brah-rah' oos-tayd', een-kloo-yayn'doh eem-pooays'tohs
ee sayr-vee'seeoh?*
What price will you charge, including tax and service?

¿Podría usted hacerme una rebaja?
poh-dree'ah oos-tayd' ah-sayr'may oo'nah ray-bah'hah?
Could you give me a slightly lower price?

Después de todo, estaré aquí tres semanas.
days-pooays' day toh'doh, ays-tah-ray' ah-kee' trays say-mah'nahs.
After all, I will be here 3 weeks.

¿Podría tener un cuarto con baño por el mismo precio?
*poh-dree'ah tay-nayr' oon kwahr'toh kohn bah-nyoh pohr ayl
mees'moh pray'seeoh?*
Can I have a room with bath for the same price?

Viviré aquí por algún tiempo.
vee-vee-ray' ah-kee' pohr ahl-goon' teeaym'poh.
I will be living here for some time.

Tome todos los mensajes.
toh'may toh'dohs lohs mayn-sah'hays.
Take all messages.

Y cuide mi correo.
ee kwee'day mee koh-rray'oh.
And look after my mail.

Si mis amigos vienen, llévelos a mi apartamento.
see mees ah-mee'gohs veeayn'nayn, yay'vay-lohs ah mee
    ah-pahr-tah-mayn'toh.
If friends call, show them to my apartment.

A fines de mes le daré una propina.
ah fee'nays day mays lay dah-ray' oo'nah proh-pee'nah.
At the end of the month, I will give you a tip.

THE SIDEWALK CAFE

¡Camarero (Mozo. Mesero)!
¡kah-mah-ray'roh (moh'soh. may-say-roh)!
Waiter!

Una cerveza, por favor.
oo'nah sayr-vay'sah, pohr fah-vohrr'.
A beer, please.

Un whisky escocés.
oon ooees'kee ays-koh-says'.
A Scotch whisky.

¿Qué jugos de frutas tiene?
kay hoo'gohs day frroo'tahs teeay'nay?
What fruit juices do you have?

Tenemos de naranja, tomate y toronja.
tay-nay'mohs day nah-rahn'hah, toh-mah'tay ee toh-rohn'hah.
We have orange, tomato and grapefruit.

Una copa de jerez.
oo'nah koh'pah day hay-rays'.
A glass of sherry.

¿Qué licores tiene?
kay lee-koh'rehs teeay'nay?
What kind of liqueurs do you have?

Un vaso de vino tinto (blanco).
oon vah'soh day vee'noh teen'toh (blahn'koh).
A glass of red (white) wine.

La cuenta, por favor.
lah kwayn'tah, pohr fah-vohrr!
The check, please.

Está incluido el servicio en la cuenta?
ays-tah' een-klooee'doh ayl sayrr-vee'seeoh ayn lah kwayn'tah?
Is the service included in the bill?

No, no está.
noh, noh ays-tah'.
No, it is not.

DINING OUT

Una mesa para dos, por favor.
oo'nah may'sah pah'rah dohs, pohr fah-vohrr'.
A table for two, please.

¿Me permite un menú, por favor?
may payr-mee'tay oon may-noo', pohr fah-vohrr'.
May I have a menu, please?

¿Sirven ustedes a la carta o comida fija?
seer'vayn oos-tray'days ah lah kahr'tah oh koh-mee'dah fee'hah?
Do you serve à la carte or table d'hôte?

Por favor, sírvanos pronto. Tenemos prisa.
pohr fah-vohrr', seer'vah-nohs prohn'-toh.
        tay-nay'mohs pree'sah.
Please serve us quickly. We are in a hurry.

¿De cuántos platos consiste?
day kwahn'tohs plah'tohs kohn-sees'tay?
How many courses are there?

¿Qué contiene este plato?
kay kohn-teeay'nay ays'tay plah'toh?
What does this dish consist of?

¿Qué recomienda usted?
kay ray-koh-mee-ayn'dah oos-tayd'?
What do you recommend?

Primero tomaremos sopa.
pree-may'roh toh-may-ray'mohs   soh'pah.
First, we'll have soup.

Mi esposa comerá esto.
mee ays-poh'sah koh-may-rah'   ays'toh.
My wife will have this.

Comenzaré con caldo.
koh-mayn-sah-ray' kohn kahl'doh.
I will start with broth.

Para el platillo principal quisiera tamales.
pah'rah eyl plah-tee'yoh preen-see-pahl kee-see-ay'rah tah-mah'lays.
For the main course I would like tamales.

Con chile, por favor.
kohn chee'lay, pohr fah-vohrr'.
With chile, please.

Sin picante, por favor.
seen pee-kan'tay, pohr fah-vohrr'.
Not hot, please.

Un limón rebanado, por favor.
oon lee-mohn' ray-bah-nah'doh, pohr fah-vohrr'.
A sliced lemon, please.

De postre quiero flan.
day pohs'tray kee-ay'roh flahn.
Let me have custard for dessert.

¿Desea beber algo, señor?
day-say'ah bay-bayrr' ahl'goh, say-nyorr'?
Would you like something to drink, sir?

Sí, un vaso de vino del país.
see, oon vah'soh day vee'noh dayl pah-ees'.
Yes, a glass of native wine.

No, nada, gracias.
noh, nah'dah, gra'see-ahs.
No, nothing, thank you.

Déme una botella de cerveza fría.
day'may oo'nah boh-tay'yah day sayr-vay'sah free'ah.
Let me have a bottle of cold beer.

Una taza de café con crema.
oo'nah tah'sah day kah-fay' kohn kray'mah.
A cup of coffee with cream.

Café solo, por favor.
kah-fay' soh'loh, pohr fah-vohrr'.
Black coffee, please.

Pan, por favor.
pahn, pohr fah-vohrr'.
Some bread, please.

Más mantequilla.
mahs mahn-tay-kee'ya.
More butter.

¿Tiene panecillos?
tee-ay'nay pah-nay-see'yohs?
Do you have any rolls?

Camarero, se le olvidó darme una servilleta.
kah-mah-ray'roh, say lay ohl-vee-doh' dahr'may oo'nah sayr-vee-yay'tah.
Waiter, you forgot to give me a napkin.

Camarero, la cuenta, por favor.
kah-mah-ray'roh, lah kwayn'tah, pohr fah-vohrr'.
Waiter, the check, please.

Creo que no ha sumado bien la cuenta.
kray'oh kay noh ah soo-mah'doh bee-ayn' lah kwayn'tah.
I think you've added up the bill incorrectly.

La revisaré otra vez, señor.
lah ray-vee-sah-ray' oh' trah vays, say-nyorr'.
I'll check it again, sir.

Tiene razón, me he equivocado.
tee-ay'nay rah-sohn' may ay ay-kee-voh-kah'doh.
You are right, I've made a mistake.

Me gustó mucho la comida.
may goos-toh' moo'choh lah koh-mee'dah.
I enjoyed the meal very much.

Con gusto recomendaré este lugar a mis amigos.
kohn goos'toh ray-koh-mayn-dah-ray' ays'tay loo-gahr' ah mees ah-mee'gohs.
I shall be glad to recommend this place to my friends.

Atienden muy bien aquí.
ah-tee-ayn'dayn moo'ee bee-ayn' ah-kee'.
The service was excellent.

NATIVE DISHES

Cocido.
koh-see'doh.
Spanish Boiled Dinner. Meat, chicken, salt pork, ham, Spanish sausages and pigs feet boiled in a pot with chick peas, cabbage and potatoes. (Regional dish, Castile.)

Caldo gallego.
kahl-doh gah-yay'goh.
Spanish national soup. Bean soup with pieces of meat, ham, Spanish sausages and vegetables. (Galicia, Spain.)

Paella valenciana.
pah-ay'yah vah-layn-seeah'nah.
Yellow rice with sea food, chicken, pork and lima beans or peas. (Valencia, Spain) [Maybe the most popular of all Spanish dishes.]

Arroz con pollo.
ah-rrohs' kohn poh'yoh.
Yellow rice with chicken.

Solomillo asado a la parrilla.
sah-loh-mee'yoh ah-sah'doh ah lah pah-rree'yah.
Grilled tenderloin, served without sauce or with many variations of sauces.

Picadillo de carne.
pee-kah-dee'yoh day kahrr'nay.
Highly-seasoned finely chopped beef and pork cooked in a sauce of
olive oil, onions, capers, olives and raisins.

Empanadas.
aym-pah-nah'dahs.
Meat pie, biscuit dough filled with chopped meat (picadillo) and
deep-fried.

Chilindrón de carnero.
chee-leen-drohn' day kahrr-nay'roh.
Mutton cooked in a dry sherry wine sauce.

Guisado de riñones de ternera.
gee-sah'doh day ree-nyoh'nays day tayrr-nay'rah.
Stew of veal kidney with Madeira wine or sweet sherry wine sauce.

Codornices a la malagueña.
koh-dohrr-nee'says ah lah mah-lah-gay'nyah.
Roasted quails stuffed with grapes, grated orange peel, raisins and
brandy. Served in its own sauce to which brandy is added
and ignited. (Málaga, Spain.)

Pollo en cazuela con legumbres.
poh'yoh ayn kah-sooay'lah kohn lay-goom'brays.
Chicken cooked in casserole with vegetables.

Lengua guisada en pepitoria.
layng'gwah gee-sah'dah ayn pay-pee-toh'reeah.
Sliced tongue or pieces of chicken served in a sauce made of white
wine, egg yolks, almonds and olives.

Pescado en escabeche.
pays-kah'doh ayn ays-kah-bay'chay.
Fried or boiled fish which has been kept for some time in a sauce
made of olive oil, vinegar, dry mustard, laurel leaves, green
peppers, salt, pepper, olives and onions. It is served cold.

Pescado en salsa verde.
pays-kah'doh ayn sahl'sah vayrr'day.
Baked fish served in a sauce whose basic ingredient is parsley.

Pescado relleno.
pays-kah'doh rray-yay'noh.
Stuffed fish, generally red snapper, boned, stuffed with vegetables and
served in tomato sauce or green sauce.

Bacalao a la vizcaína.
bah-kah-lah'oh ah lah vees-kah-ee'nah.
Pieces of salt cod fish served in an olive oil sauce with fried slices of bread and hard boiled eggs. (Basque country)

Calamares en su tinta.
kah-lah-mah'rays ayn soo teen'tah.
Fresh squid served in a red wine sauce and its own "ink".

Hongos rellenos con almendras.
ohn'gohs rray-yay'nohs kohn ahl-mayn'drahs.
Grilled mushroom caps filled with a paste of grated mushrooms, almonds, butter, onions, lemon juice and sherry wine.

Tortilla a la española.
tohrr-tee'yah ah lah ays-pah-nyoh'lah.
Omelet with potatoes (not with tomato sauce).

Guacamole.
gooah-kah-moh'lay.
Mashed avocado seasoned with tomato, olive oil, finely chopped onions, salt and pepper. Served as hors d'oeuvres on potato chips or "tortillas" (Mexican pancakes). Very popular in South America, not in Spain.

Frijoles negros.
free-joh'lays nay'grohs.
Black beans. Generally served with white rice. (Spanish America).

Plátanos fritos (maduros, verdes).
plah'tah-nohs frree'tohs (mah-doo'rohs, vayr'days).
Fried bananas (ripe, green). These are the big bananas (plantains) used for cooking.

SIGHTSEEING AND AMUSEMENTS

¿Cómo se va a León, por favor?
koh'moh say vah ah lay-ohn', pohr fah-vohrr'?
What is the way to León, please?

Lléveme a Quito.
yay-vay-may ah kee'toh.
Take me to Quito.

Más despacio, por favor. No tengo prisa.
mahs days-pah'see-oh pohr fah-vohrr'. noh tayn'goh pree'sah.
Slower, please. I'm in no hurry.

Más rápido, por favor. Tengo prisa.
mahs rah'pee-doh pohr fah-vohrr'. tayn'goh pree'sah.
Faster, please. I'm in a hurry.

¿Qué es ese edificio que estamos pasando?
kay ays ay'say ay-dee-fee'see-oh kay ays-tah'mohs
          pah-sahn'doh?
What is this building we are passing?

¿Tiene un fósforo?
tee-ay'nay oon fohs'foh-roh?
Do you have a match?

¿Habrá buenas corridas este domingo?
ah-brah' boo-ay'nahs koh-rree'dahs ays'tay doh-meen'goh?
Will there be good bullfights this Sunday?

¿Cuánto me cobra por un viaje a Taxco?
kwahn-toh may koh'brah pohr oon veeah'hay ah tahs'koh?
How much will you charge for a trip to Taxco?

Es demasiado.
ays day-mah-see-ah'doh.
That is too much.

Entiendo que cincuenta pesos es suficiente.
ayn tee-ayn'doh kay seen-kooayn'tah pay'sohs ays soo-fee-see-ayn'tay.
I understand that 50 pesos is enough.

Muy bien, lo llevaré por esa cantidad.
moo'ee bee-ayn', loh yay-vah-ray' pohr ay'sah kahn-tee-dahd'.
Very well, I will take you for that amount.

¿Va esta línea al Castillo?
vah ays'tah lee'nay-ah ahl kahs-tee'yoh?
Does this line go to Castillo?

¿Cuánto cuesta el pasaje?
kwan'toh kways'tah ayl pah-sah'hay?
How much is the fare?

¿Este autobús (tranvía) se detiene en el Zócalo?
ays'tay ahoo-toh-boos' (trahn-vee'ah) say day-teeay'nay ayn ayl [soh'kah-loh?
Does this bus (trolley) stop at Zocalo?

Bullfights

Dos boletos para el domingo.
dohs boh-lay'tohs pah'rah ayl doh-meen'goh.
Two tickets for Sunday.

¿Tiene usted todavía boletos de sombra?
tee-ay'nay oos-tayd' toh-dah-vee'ah boh-lay'tohs day sohm'brah?
Do you still have some seats on the shady side?

No, señor, sólo tengo asientos de palco.
noh, say-nyohr', soh'loh tayn-goh ah-seeayn'tohs day pahl'koh.
No, sir, I only have box seats left.

¿Cuánto cuesta un boleto de barrera?
kwahn'toh kways'tah oon boh-lay'toh day bah-ray'rah?
How much is the admission to ringside?

¿Va este autobús a la plaza de toros?
vah ays'tay ahoo-toh-boos' ah lah plah'sah day toh'rohs?
Does this bus go to the bullring?

Taxi, a la plaza de toros, por favor.
tahk'see, ah lah plah'sah day toh'rohs, pohr fah-vohrr'.
Taxi, to the bullring, please.

Por favor, aprisa. Son casi las cuatro.
pohr fah-vohrr', ah-pree'sah. sohn kah'see lahs kwah'troh.
Please hurry. It's almost four o'clock.

Jai-Alai

¿A qué hora comienza el jai-alai?
ah kay' oh'rah koh-mee-ayn'sah ayl hah'ee-ah-lah'ee?
At what time does the jai-alai start?

Dos boletos de diez pesos, por favor.
dohs boh-lay'tohs day dee'ays' pay'sohs, pohr fah-vohrr'.
Two ten peso tickets, please.

¿En qué fila están?
ayn kay fee'lah ays-tahn'?
In what row are they?

Lotteries

Un pedazo de billete de lotería.
oon pay-dah'soh day bee-yay'tay day loh-tay-ree'ah.
A portion of a lottery ticket.

¿Es para un sorteo especial?
ays pah'rah oon sohr-tay'oh ays-pay-see-ahl'?
Is it for a special drawing?

¿Puedo ver la lista de la lotería?
pway'doh vayr lah lees'tah day lah loh-tay-ree'ah?
May I see the lottery list?

Déme un número con suerte.
day'may oon noo'may-roh kohn swayr'tay.
Give me a lucky number.

¿Cuánto es el primer premio?
kwahn'toh ays ayl pree-mayr' pray'mee-oh?
How much is the first prize?

Creo que me saqué algo en la lotería.
kray'oh kay may sah-kay' ahl'goh ayn lah loh-tay-ree'ah.
I think I've won something in the lottery.

¿Dónde puedo cobrarlo?
dohn'day pway'doh koh-brahr'loh?
Where can I cash it?

¿Cuánto es mi premio?
kwahn'toh ays mee pray'mee-oh?
How much is my prize?

Horseracing

¿Por dónde se va a la tribuna?
pohr dohn'day say vah ah lah tree-boo'nah?
Which way to the grandstand?

Dos boletos para el club, por favor.
dohs boh-lay'tohs pah'rah ayl kloob, pohr fah-vohrr'.
Two tickets for the club house, please.

¿Dónde puedo apostar?
dohn'day pway'doh ah-pohs-tahr'?
Where can I place a bet?

¿Cuál es el favorito?
kwahl ays ayl fah-voh-ree'toh?
Which is the favorite?

Los caballos están llegando a la barrera de salida.
lohs kah-bah'yohs ays-tahn' yay-gahn'doh ah lah bah-ray'rah day sah-lee'dah.
The horses are approaching the starting gate.

Su caballo gana.
soo kah-bah'yoh gah'nah.
Your horse wins.

Gambling

Hagan sus apuestas, por favor.
ah'gahn soos ah-pways'tahs,
pohr fah-vohrr'.
Place your bets, please.

Un dólar al negro (al rojo).
oon doh'lahr ahl nay'groh
(ahl roh'hoh).
One dollar on black (on red).

Carnival

¿Va a salir en el desfile?
vah ah sah-leer' ayn ayl days-fee'lay?
Will you take part in the parade?

¿Cómo podemos salir? No tenemos disfraces.
koh-moh poh-day'mohs sah-leer'? non tay-nay'mohs dees-frah'says.
How can we? We have no costumes.

¿Por qué no compramos asientos en la tribuna?
pohr kay noh kohm-prah'mohs ah-see-ayn'tohs ayn lah tree-boo'nah?
Why don't we get seats in the stands?

Regatta

¿Cuándo comienza la regata?
kwahn'doh koh-mee-ayn'sah lah ray-gah'tah?
When does the regatta start?

¿Puede verse desde aquí?
pway'day vayr'say days'day ah-kee'?
Can it be seen from here?

SNAPSHOTS FOR REMEMBRANCE

¿Tiene la amabilidad de permitir que la retrate?
tee-ay-nay lah ah-mah-bee-lee-dahd' day payr-mee-teer' kay
lah ray-trah'tay?
Would you be good enough to pose for a photograph?

Por favor párese allá.
pohr fah-vohrr' pah'ray-say ah-yah'.
Please stand over there.

No mire la cámara.
noh mee'ray lah kah'mah-rah.
Don't look at the camera.

Dése vuelta hacia acá, por favor.
day'say vooayl'tah ah'see-ah ah-kah', pohr fah-vohrr'.
Turn this way, please.

Quisiera darle esto por haberse molestado.
*kee-see-ay'rah dahr'lay ays'toh pohr ah-bayr'say
        moh-lays-tah'-doh.*
I'd like you to have this for your trouble.

Gracias, es usted muy amable.
grah'see-ahs, ays oos-tayd' moo'ee ah-mah'blay.
Thanks, it's very kind of you.

Lleve estos dulces a sus niños.
yay'vay ays'tohs dool'says ah soos nee'nyohs.
Take this candy for your children.

Quiero que me revelen este rollo de película.
*kee-ay'roh kay may ray-vay'layn ays'tay
        roh-yoy day pay-lee-koo-lah.*
I'd like to have this roll of film developed.

Por favor, haga una copia de cada negativo.
*pohr fah-vohrr' ah'gah oo'nah koh'pee-ah day kah'dah
        nay-gah-tee'voh.*
Please make one print of each negative.

Deseo una ampliación de cada fotografía.
*day-say'oh oo'nah ahm-plee-ah-seeohn' day kah-dah
        foh-toh-grah-fee'ah.*
I would like an enlargement of each picture.

¿Cuánto tardará?
kwahn'toh tahr-dah-rah'?
How long will it take?

Déme un rollo de película número ocho.
day'may oon roh'yoh day pay-lee'koo-lah, noo'may-roh oh'choh.
Let me have a roll of film, number 8.

Quisiera un rollo de película a color.
kee-see-ay'-rah oon roh'yoh day pay-lee'koo-lah ah koh-lohr'.
I would like a roll of color film.

Déme una docena de focos "flash".
day'may oo'nah doh-say'nah day foh'kohs "flahsh".
Let me have a dozen flashbulbs.

Un rollo de película de ocho milímetros para cine.
oon roh'yoh day oh'cho mee-lee'may-trohs pah'rah see'nay.
A roll of 8 mm. movie film.

¿Tiene película para cine de dieciseis milímetros?
tee-ay'nay pay-lee'koo-lah pah'rah see'nay day
   dee-ays'see-says mee-lee'may-trohs?
Do you have 16mm. movie film?

En blanco y negro. En rollo. En magazine.
ayn nay'groh ee blahn'koh. ayn roh'yoh. ayn mah-gah-seen'.
Black and white. On a roll. In a magazine.

El precio incluye el revelado?
ayl pray'-see-oh een-kloo'yay ayl ray-vay-lah'doh?
Does the price include processing?

¿Quiere hacer el favor de ponerme el rollo?
kee-ay'ray ah-sayr' ayl fah-vohrr' day poh-nayr'may ayl
   roh'yoh?
Will you load the camera for me, please?

El diafragma no funciona. ¿Quiere examinarlo?
ayl dee-ah-frahg'mah noh foon-see'oh' nah.
   kee-ay'ray ayk-sah-mee-nahr'loh.
The shutter is stuck. Will you please look at it?

¿Por qué se me raya la película?
pohr-kay' say may rah'yah lah pay-lee'koo-lah?
Why does my film get scratched?

¿Cree usted que debo usar un filtro?
kray oos-tayd' kay day-boh oo-sahr' oon feel'troh?
Do you think I should use a filter?

SHOPPING WITH ASSURANCE

¿Cuánto cuesta esto?
kwahn'toh kways'tah ays'toh?
How much is this?

Es demasiado.
ays day-mah-see-ah'doh.
That is too much.

Si me hace una rebaja compraré más cosas.
see may ah'say oo'nah ray-bah'hah kohm-prah-ray'
   mahs koh'sahs.
If you make a reduction I will buy more things.

Esta es muy grande (chica).
ays'tah ays moo'ee grahn'day (chee'kah).
This is too large (small).

Esta es muy estrecha (ancha).
ays'tah ays moo'ee ays-tray'chah (ahn'chah).
This is too tight (loose).

¿Tiene algo mejor?
tee-ay'nay ahl'goh may-hohrr'?
Have you anything better?

¿Tiene usted un ejemplar de "Esta Semana"?
*tee-ay'nay oos-tayd' oon ay-hem-plahr' day ays'tah
        say-mah'nah?*
Do you have a copy of "This Week"?

¿Dónde puedo comprar un diario en inglés?
dohn'day pway'doh kohm-prahrr' oon dee-ah'ree-oh ayn ee-glays'?
Where can I buy an English-language daily paper?

Deseo ver unos artículos de lana.
day-say'oh vairr oo'nohs ahr-tee'koo-lohs day lah'nah.
I would like to see some of your woolen goods.

¿Tiene esto en color más claro (oscuro)?
*tee-ay'nay ays'toh ayn koh-lohrr' mahs klah'roh
        (ohs-koo'roh)?*
Do you have this in a lighter (darker) color?

¿Cuánto cuesta el metro (la yarda)?
kwan'toh kways'tah ayl meh'tro (lah yahr'dah)?
How much is this a meter (a yard)?

¿Qué tiene para un niño (una niña) de cinco años?
*kay tee-ay'nay pah'rah oon nee'nyoh (oo'nah nee'nyah) day
        seen'koh ah'nyohs?*
What do you have for a five year old?

¿Tiene usted vestidos bordados?
tee-ay'nay oos-tayd' vays-tee'dohs bohr-dah'dohs?
Do you have embroidered dresses?

¿Cuánto cuesta ese saco de ante?
kwan'toh kways'tah ay'say sah'koh day ahn'tay?
What is the price of that suède jacket?

¿Es ésta una tela importada?
ays ays'tah oo'nah tay'lah eem-pohr-tah'dah?
Is this an imported fabric?

¿En qué país se hizo?
ayn kay pah-ees' say ee'soh?
In what country was it made?

¿Cuánto cuesta este perfume?
kwahn'toh kways'tah ays'tay payr-foo'may?
What is the price of this perfume?

No me gusta este dibujo.
noh may goos'tah ays'tay dee-boo'hoh.
I don't like this design.

¿Cuánto cuestan estos aretes?
kwan'toh kways'tah ays'tohs ah-ray'tays?
What is the price of these earrings?

Permítame ver esa pulsera, por favor.
payr-mee'tah-may vayr ay'sah pool-say'rah pohr fah-vohrr'.
Let me see that bracelet, please.

¿Es de plata pura esta bandeja?
ays day plah'tah poo'rah ays'tah bahn-day'hah?
Is this tray sterling silver?

Enséñeme una bandeja de plata.
ayn-say'nyay-may oo'nah bahn-day'hah day plah'tah.
Show me a silver tray.

Se hacen artículos de plata al gusto, verdad?
*say ah'sayn ahr-tee'coo-lohs day plah'tah ahl goos'toh,
    vayr-dad'?*
You make silver articles to order, don't you?

Enséñeme un rebozo de seda.
ayn-say'nyay-may oon ray-boh'soh day say'dah.
Let me see a silk rebozo.

Me gusta el negro de rayón.
may goos'tah ayl nay'groh day rah-yohn'.
I like the black rayon one.

¿Qué largo tiene el rojo?
kay lahr'goh teeay'nay ayl roh'hoh?
How long is the red one?

¿Tiene esta camisa en azul?
tee-ay'nay ays'tah kah-mee'sah ayn ah-sool'?
Do you have this shirt in blue?

¿Tiene usted mi tamaño en verde?
tee-ay'nay oos-tayd' mee tah-mah'nyoh ayn vayr'day?
Do you have my size in green?

Deseo comprar un sarape grande, para cama.
day-say'oh kohm-prahrr' oon sah-rah'pay grahn'day, pah'rah kah'mah.
I want to buy a large sarape for a bed.

¿Dónde se venden los artículos de cuero?
dohn'day say vayn'dayn lohs ahr-tee'koo-lohs day kway'roh?
Where is the leather goods counter?

Tome el elevador al segundo piso.
toh'may ayl el-lay-vah-dohr' ahl say-goon'doh pee'soh.
Take the elevator to the second floor.

Por favor llame a un dependiente.
pohr fah-vohrr' ya'may ah oon day-payn-dee-ayn'tay.
Will you please get me a clerk.

Quisiera ver un vestido de lino bordado.
kee-see-ay'rah vayr oon vays-tee'doh day lee'noh bohr-dah'doh.
I would like to see an embroidered linen dress.

¿Tiene usted una guayabera en mi talla?
tee-ay'nay oos-tayd' oo'nah gwah-yah-bay'rah ayn mee tah'yah?
Do you have a guayabera in my size?

¿Cuánto cuesta esa bolsa de cocodrilo?
kwahn'toh kways'tah ay'sah bohl'sah day koh-koh-dree'loh?
What is the price of that alligator handbag?

¿Es hecho a mano?
ays ay'choh ah mah'noh?
Is this hand made?

Me llevaré este cinturón.
may yay-vah-ray' ays'tay seen-too-rohn'.
I will take this belt.

¿Cuánto cuesta esta botella de ron?
kwahn'toh kways'tah ays'tah boh-tay'yah day rohn?
How much is this bottle of rum?

¿Qué clase de licores tiene?
kay clah'say day lee-koh'rays tee-ay'nay?
What kind of cordials do you carry?

Me gustaría probar algo menos dulce.
may goos-tah-ree'ah proh-bahr' ahl'goh may'nohs dool'say.
I would like to try something less sweet.

Déme una caja de puros tamaño panetela.
day'me oo'nah kah-hah day poo'rohs tah-mah'nyo pah-nay-tay'lah.
Give me a box of cigars in the panatella size.

Son muy fuertes estos cigarros (puros)?
sohn moo'ee fwayr'tays ays'tohs see-gah'rohs (poo'rohs)?
Are these cigars very strong?

¿Cómo se llama esta marca?
koh'moh say yah'mah ays'tah mahr'kah?
What is the name of this brand?

Por favor empáquelo en una caja.
pohr fah-vohrr' aym-pah'kay-loh ayn oo'nah kah'hah.
Please pack it in a box.

Aquí está su bulto, señora.
ah-kee' ays-tah' soo bool'toh, say-nyoh'rah.
Here is your package, madam.

Mándemelo a mi hotel, por favor.
mahn'day-may-loh ah mee oh-tayl', pohr fah-vohrr'.
Send it to my hotel, please.

Por favor, déme una factura para esta compra.
*pohr fah-vohrr' day'may oo'nah fahk-too'rah pah'rah
      ays'tah kohm'prah.*
Please let me have a sales slip for this purchase.

No deje de enviármelo por correo inmediatamente.
*noh-day'hay day ayn-vee-ahr'may-loh pohr koh-ray'oh
      een-may-dee-ah-tah-mayn'tay.*
Be sure to mail it immediately.

Mi dirección es Paseo de la Reforma No. 15.
mee dee-rayk-see-ohn' ays pah-say'oh day lah ray-fohr'mah noo'may-roh
My address is 15 Paseo de la Reforma.   *[keen'say.*

LAUNDRY AND CLEANING

Por favor, lave este vestido.
pohr fah-vohrr', lah'vay ays'tay vays-tee'doh.
Please wash this dress.

Sin almidón, por favor.
seen ahl-mee-dohn' pohr fah-vohrr'.
Without starch, please.

Quiero este traje lavado en seco.
kee-ay'roh ays'tay trah'hay lah-vah-doh ayn say'koh.
I want this suit dry cleaned.

¿Cuándo estará listo?
kwahn-doh ays-tah-rah' lees'toh?
When can you have it ready?

Lo necesito mañana.
loh nay-say-see'toh ma-nyah'nah.
I must have it tomorrow.

Por favor, planche estos pantalones.
pohr fah-vohrr' plahn'chay ays'tohs pahn-tah-loh'nays.
Please press these trousers.

Está roto. ¿Puede arreglarlo?
ays-tah' roh'toh pway'day ah-ray-glahr'loh?
This is torn. Can you mend it?

HAIRDRESSERS AND BARBERS

Deseo un corte de pelo a las once.
day-say'-oh oon kohr'tay day pay'loh ah lahs ohn'say.
I'd like to have a haircut at 11 o'clock.

Deseo una cita para manicure.
day-say' oh oo'nah see'tah pah'rah mah-nee-kee-oor'.
I would like to make an appointment for a manicure.

¿A qué hora puede recibirme para un champú?
ah kay or'rah pway'day ray-see-beer'may pah'rah oon chahm-poo'?
What time can you take me for a shampoo?

Un ligero corte, por favor.
oon lee-hay'roh kohr'tay pohr fah-vohrr'.
A trim, please.

Un corte a cepillo.
oon kohr'tay ah say-pee'yoh.
A crew cut.

No me corte mucho arriba.
noh may kohr'tay moo'choh ah-ree'bah.
Not too much off the top.

Más corto, por favor.
mahs kohr'toh, pohr fah-vohrr'.
Make it shorter, please.

GOING TO CHURCH

Quisiera ir a la iglesia.
kee-seeay'rah eerr ah lah ee-glay'seeah.
I would like to go to church.

¿En dónde está la iglesia (más cercana)?
ayn dohn'day ays-tah' lah ee-glay'seeah (mas' sayrr-kah'nah)?
Where is the (nearest) church?

¿En dónde está la Catedral?
ayn dohn'day ays-tah' lah kah-tay-drahl'?
Where is the cathedral?

¿En dónde está la sinagoga?
ayn dohn'day ays-tah' lah see-nah-goh'gah?
Where is the synagogue?

¿Qué clase de iglesia es ésta?
kay klah'say day ee-glay'seeah ays ays'tah?
What kind of a church is this?

Una iglesia católica.
oo'nah ee-glay'seeah kah-toh'lee-kah.
A Catholic church.

Una iglesia protestante.
oo'nah ee-glay'seeah proh-tays-tahn'tay.
A Protestant church.

¿A qué hora empieza la misa?
ah kay oh'rah aym-peeay'sah lah mee'sah?
At what time does the mass start?

¿Qué iglesia celebra los oficios en inglés?
kay ee-glay'seeah say-lay brrah lohs oh-fee'seeohs ayn een-glays'?
What church holds service in English?

¿Podemos asistir a este oficio?
poh-day'mohs ah-sees-teerr' ah ays'tay oh-fee'seeoh?
May we attend this service?

Quisiera ver a un ministro (sacerdote, rabí).
kee-seeay'rah vayrr' ah oon mee-nees'trroh (sah-sayrr-doh'tay rrah-bee').
I would like to see a minister (priest, rabbi).

THEATER GOING

Desearía dos billetes para mañana.
day-say-ah-ree'ah dohs bee-yay'tays pah'rah mah-nyah'nah.
I should like two tickets for tomorrow.

¿Tiene usted asientos para esta noche?
teeay'nay oos-tayd' ah-seeayn'tohs pah'rah ays'tah noh'chay?
Have you any seats for tonight?

¿En dónde están los asientos?
ayn dohn'day ays-tahn' lohs ah-seeayn'tohs?
Where are the seats located?

¿Puede usted mostrarme un plano de los asientos del teatro?
pooay'day oos-tayd' mohs-trahrr'may oon plah-noh day lohs ah-seeayn'tohs dayl tay-ah'troh?
   Can you show me a seating plan of the theater?

Por favor, deme dos butacas (asientos de platea, palco, galería).
pohr fah-vohrr' day-may dohs boo-tah'kahs (ah-seeayn'tohs day plah-tay'ah, pahl'koh, gah-lay-ree'ah).
Please let me have two orchestra (mezzanine, box, balcony) seats.

¿A qué hora empieza la función?
ah kay oh'rah aym-peeay'sah lah foon-seeohn'?
At what time does the performance start?

NIGHT LIFE

Deseo visitar algunos cabarets.
day-say'oh vee-see-tahr' ahl-goo'nohs kah-bah-rayts'.
I want to visit several night clubs.

Me gustaría ver algunas buenas funciones.
may goo-stah-ree'ah vayrr' ahl-goo'nahs booay'nahs foon-seeoh'nays.
I would like to see some good floor shows.

¿Qué sitios recomienda usted?
kay see'teeohs ray-koh-meeayn'dah oos-tayd'?
What places do you recommend?

¿Son muy caros?
sohn mooee kah-rohs?
Are they very expensive?

¿Cobran por la admisión?
koh'brahn pohr lah ahd-mee-seeohn'?
Is there a cover charge?

¿Cobran por alguna otra cosa?
koh'brahn pohr ahl-goo'nah oh'trah koh'sah?
Are there any other charges?

¿A qué hora comienza la función?
ah kay oh'rah koh-meeayn'sah lah foon-seeohn'?
What time does the floor show start?

Hay una equivocación en la cuenta.
ahee oo'nah ay-kee-voh-kah-seeohn' ayn lah kwayn'tah.
There is an error in the bill.

Por favor, haga corregir la cuenta.
pohr fah-vohrr', ah'gah koh-rray-heer' lah kwayn'tah.
Please see that my bill is corrected.

EXCHANGING MONEY

Deseo cambiar este cheque de viajero.
*day-say'oh kahm-bee-ahr' ays'tay chay'kay day
        vee-ah-hey'roh.*
I should like to cash this travelers check.

¿Me puede dar pesos por este billete de diez dólares?
*may pooay'day dahr pay'sohs pohr ays'tay bee-yay'tay day deeays'
        doh'lah-rays?*
May I have pesos for this ten dollar bill?

¿Dónde puedo comprar un giro bancario?
*dohn'day pway'doh kohm-prahr' oon hee'roh
        bahn-kah'ree-oh?*
Where can I buy a bank draft?

En la siguiente ventanilla.
ayn lah see-ghee-ayn'tay vayn-tah-nee'yah.
At the next window.

COMMUNICATIONS

Post Office

¿Dónde está el correo?
dohn'day ays-tah' ayl koh-ray'oh?
Where is the post office?

¿Hasta qué hora está abierto?
ahs'tah kay oh'rah ays-tah' ah-bee-ayr'toh?
Until what time is it open?

Se cierra a las cinco.
say see-ay'rah ah lahs seen'koh.
It closes at five o'clock.

¿Dónde puedo comprar unos sellos?
dohn'day pway'doh kohm-prahr' oo'nohs say'yohs?
Where can I buy some stamps?

En la ventanilla número 4.
any lah vayn-tah-nee'yah noo'may-roh kooah'troh.
At window number 4.

Déme un sello aéreo, por favor.
day'may oon say'yoh ah-ay'ray-oh pohr fah-vohrr'.
Let me have an airmail stamp, please.

Quiero enviar ésta entrega inmediata.
kee'ay'roh ayn-vee'ahr' ays'tah ayn-tray'-gah
            een-may-dee-ah'tah.
I want to send this special delivery.

¿Cuánto es el franqueo de esta carta?
kwahn'toh ays ayl frahn-kay'oh day ays'tah kahr'tah?
How much postage do I need on this letter?

Deseo certificar esta carta.
day-say'oh sayr-tee-fee-kahr' ays'tah kahr'tah.
I would like to register this letter.

¿Puedo asegurar este bulto?
pway'doh ah-say-goo-rahr' ays'tay bool'toh?
May I insure this parcel?

¿Qué contiene?
kay kohn-tee-ay'nay?
What does it contain?

Libros e impresos.
lee'brohs ay eem-pray'sohs.
Books and printed matter.

Guarde mi correspondencia hasta que yo venga.
gwahr'day mee koh-rays-pohn-dayn'seeah ahs'tah kay yoh vayn'gah.
Hold my mail until I call for it.

Por favor mande mi correspondencia a Nueva York.
pohr fah-vorr' mahn'day mee koh-rays-pohn-dayn'seeah ah nooay'vah
Please forward my mail to New York. [*yohrk'.*

No se moleste en mandarme revistas y periódicos.
*noh say moh-lays'tay ayn mahn-dahr'may ray-vees'tahs ee
pay-ree-oh'dee-kohs.*
Don't bother to send magazines and newspapers.

Telephoning

¿Dónde está el teléfono más cercano?
dohn'day ays-tah' ayl tay-lay'foh-noh mahs sayr-kah'noh?
Where is the nearest telephone?

Oigo, habla Roberto.
ohee'goh, ah'blah roh-bayr'toh.
Hello, this is Robert calling.

¿Está Luis allí?
ays-tah' looees' ah-yee'?
Is Louis there?

No está.
noh ays-tah'.
He is not in.

No cuelgue, por favor. Lo llamaré.
noh kwayl'gay, pohr fah-vohrr'. loh yah-mah-ray'.
Hold the wire, please. I'll put him on.

¿Puedo dejar un recado?
pway'doh day-hahr' oon ray-kah'doh?
May I leave a message, please?

¿A qué hora lo espera?
ah kay oh'rah loh ays-pay'rah?
When is he expected?

Deseo hacer una llamada de larga distancia.
day-say'oh ah-sayr' oo'nah yah-mah'dah day lahr'gah dees-tahn'seeah.
I want to make a long distance call.

Deseo llamar a Chicago a las tres de la tarde.
day-say'oh yah-mahr' ah chee-kah'goh ah lahs trays day lah tahr'day.
I would like to call Chicago at three o'clock.

¿Cuánto cuesta una llamada a Nueva York?
kwahn'toh kways'tah oo'nah yah-mah'dah ah nway'vah yohrk?
How much is a call to New York?

Es una llamada de teléfono a teléfono.
ays oo'nah yah-mah'dah day tay-lay'foh-noh ah tay-lay'foh- noh.
This is a station-to-station call.

Lo siento. Todas las líneas están ocupadas.
*loh see-ayn'toh toh'dahs lahs lee'nay-ahs ays-tahn' oh-koo-
        pah'-dahs.*
I'm sorry. All the lines are busy.

Dígale que el señor Cervantes está llamando de México.
*dee'gah-lay kay ayl say-nyohr sayr-vahn'tays ays-tah' yah-mahn'doh day
        may'hee-koh*
Tell him Mr. Cervantes is calling from Mexico.

Avíseme cuando terminen los tres minutos.
*ah-vee'say-may kwahn'doh tayr-mee'nayn lohs trays
        mee-noo'tohs.*
Signal me when the three minutes are over.

Por favor no interrumpa.
pohr fah-vohrr' noh een-tay-room'pah.
Please do not interrupt.

Telegrams and Cables

Deseo mandar un telegrama.
day-say'oh mahn-dahr' oon tay-lay-grah'mah.
I want to send a telegram.

Por favor, déme una hoja para escribir un cablegrama.
*pohr fah-vohr', day'may oo'nah oh'jah pah'rah ays-cree-beer'
        oon kah-blay-grah'mah.*
Please give me a blank for a foreign telegram.

¿Cuánto cuesta cada palabra?
kwahn'toh kways'tah kah'dah pah-lah'brah?
What is the rate per word?

Tiene aquí más de diez palabras.
tee-ay'nay ah-kee' mahs day dee-ays' pah-lah'-brahs.
You have more than ten words here.

Pagaré la diferencia.
pah-gah-ray' lah dee-fay-rayn'see-ah.
I shall pay for the difference.

TOURIST INFORMATION

¿En dónde está la oficina de turismo más cercana?
ayn dohn'day ays-tah' lah of-fee-see'nah day too-rees'moh mahs'
       sayr-kah'nah?
Where is the nearest tourist office?

¿Cuál es el próximo autobús para La Habana?
kwahl' ays ayl proh'gzee-moh ahoo-toh-boos'pah'rah lah ah-van-nah?
What is the next bus for Havana?

¿Qué plato regional recomienda usted?
kay plah'toh ray-heeoh-nahl' ray-koh-meeayn'da oos-tayd'?
What local food do you recommend?

Deseo visitar un lugar en que no haya turistas.
day-say'oh vee-see-tahr' oon loo-gahr' ayn kay noh ay'yah too-rees'tahs.
I wish to visit a place where there are no tourists.

Tengo muchos elegidos. Por ejemplo Alvarado.
tayn'goh moo'chohs ay-lay-hee'dohs. pohr ay-haym'ploh ahl-vah-rah'
I have many choices. For example, there is Alvarado.   [doh.

¿Está esta ciudad fuera de los caminos concurridos?
ays-tah' ays'tah seeoo-dahd' fooay'rah day lohs kah-mee'nohs
       kohn-koo-rree'dohs?
Is this town off the beaten track?

Sí, así es. (Sí, muy cierto).
see, as-see' ays. (see, mooee seeayr'toh).
Yes, very much.

¿Es difícil llegar a ese pueblo?
ays dee-fee'seel yay-gahr ah ay'say pooay'bloh?
Is it difficult to reach that village?

No, los autobuses pasan a menudo.
noh, lohs ahoo-toh-boo'says pah'sahn ah may-noo'doh.
No, there is frequent bus service.

¿Tienen allí un hotel bueno y barato?
teeay'nayn ah-yee' oon oh-tayl' booay'noh ee bah-rah'toh?
Does it have a good, inexpensive hotel?

Seguro. Recomendamos el Hotel Vista Hermosa.
say-goo'roh. ray-kho-mayn-dah'mohs ayl oh-tayl' vees'tah ayr-moh'sah.
Certainly. We recommend the Hotel Vista Hermosa.

YOUR HEALTH ABROAD

No me siento bien.
noh may see-ayn'toh bee-ayn'.
I don't feel well.

Aire, por favor.
ah'ee-ray, pohr fah-vohrr'.
Let me have some air.

Necesito un doctor.
nay-say-see'toh oon dohk-tohr'.
I need a doctor.

Tengo calentura.
tayn'goh kah-layn-too'rah.
I have a fever.

Tengo un fuerte catarro.
tayn'goh oon foo-ayr'tay kah-tah'roh.
I have a bad cold.

Me corté.
may kohr-tay'.
I cut myself.

¿Dónde está la farmacia más cercana?
dohn'day ays-tah' lah fahr-mah'see-ah mahs sayr-kah'nah?
Where is the nearest drugstore?

Por favor prepáreme esta receta.
pohr fah-vohrr' pray-pah'ray-may ays'tah ray-say'tah.
Please make up this prescription.

Aspirina.
ahs-pee-ree'nah.
Aspirin.

Bandaid.
bahnd-ah'eed.
Bandaid.

Loción para broncear.
loh-see-ohn' pah'rah brohn-say-ahr'.
Suntan lotion.

Yodo.
yoh'doh.
Iodine.

Bromo Seltzer.
broh'moh sayl'sayr.
Bromo Seltzer.

Acido bórico.
ah'see-doh boh'ree-koh.
Boric acid.

Algodón absorbente.
ahl-goh-dohn' ahb-sohr-bayn'tay.
Absorbent cotton.

Pomada de óxido de zinc.
poh-mah'dah day ohk'see-doh day seenk.
Zinc salve.

Loción contra insectos.
loh-see-ohn' kohn'trah een-sayk'tohs.
Insect repellent.

Loción contra quemaduras de sol.
loh-see-ohn' kohn'trah kay-mah-doo'rahs day sohl.
Sunburn lotion.

SPORTS

Golf

Deseo alquilar unos palos de golf, por favor.
day-say'oh ahl-kee-lahr' oo'nohs pah'lohs day gohlf, pohr fah-vohrr'.
I would like to rent a set of golf clubs, please.

¿Quiere contratar a un caddy?
kee-ay'ray kohn-trah-tahr' ah oon kah'dee?
Will you want to hire a caddy?

¿Dónde está la plataforma de salida?
dohn'day ays-tah' lah plah-tah-fohr'mah day sah-lee'dah?
Where do I tee off?

Caddy, mi palo número uno.
kah'dee, mee pah'loh noo'may-roh oo'noh.
Caddy, my driver, please.

Swimming

Deseo alquilar una sombrilla de playa.
day-say'oh ahl-kee-lahr' oo'nah sohm-bree'yah day plah'yah.
I would like to rent a beach umbrella.

¿Dónde podemos ponernos nuestro traje de baño?
dohn'day poh-day'mohs poh-nayr'nohs nways'troh
trah'hay day bahn'yoh?
Where can we change into our bathing suits?

¿Dónde puedo comprar una loción para el sol?
dohn'day pway'doh kohm-prahr' oo'nah loh-see'ohn'
pah'rah ayl sohl?
Where can I buy some suntan lotion?

Calienta mucho el sol hoy.
kah-lee-ayn'tah moo'choh ayl sohl oh'ee.
The sun is awfully strong, today.

Fishing and Hunting

Necesito una caña y carrete, cordel y anzuelos.
nay-say-see'toh oo'nah kah'nya ee kah-ray'tay, kohr-dayl' ee
ahn-soo ay'lohs.
I need a rod and reel, some line, and hooks.

¿Dónde podemos alquilar un bote (lancha)?
dohn'day poh-day'mohs ahl-kee-lahr' oon boh'tay (lahn'chah)?

Where can we rent a boat?

¿Dónde podemos pescar barracuda?
dohn'day poh-day mohs pays--cahr' bah-rah-koo'dah?

Where can we fish for barracuda?

¿Dónde puedo comprar cartuchos?
dohn'day pway'doh kohm-prahr' kahr-too'chohs?

Where can I buy ammunition?

La estación para perdices es de diciembre a marzo.
lah ays-tah-see-ohn' pah-rah payr-dee'says ays day dee-see-aym'bray ah mahr'soh.

The partridge season is from December to March.

CONDUCTING BUSINESS

Represento a una compañía americana.
ray-pray-sayn'toh ah oo'nah kohm-pah-nyee'ah ah-may-ree-kah'nah.

I represent an American firm.

Soy agente viajero.
soh'ee ah-hayn'tay vee-ah-hay'roh.

I am a traveling salesman.

Estoy aquí para conocer el mercado.
ays-toy' ah-kee' pah'rah koh-noh-sayr' ayl mayr-kah'doh.

I am here to survey the market.

Necesito un distribuidor local para mi producto.
nay-say-see'toh oon dees-tree-bwee-dohr' loh-kahl' pah-rah mee proh-dook'toh.

I need a local distributor for my product.

¿Se puede manufacturar este producto aquí?
say pway'day mah-noo-fahk-too-rahr' ays'tay proh-dook'toh ah-kee'?

Can this product be manufactured here?

OUTLINE OF SPANISH GRAMMAR

Although, for purposes of everyday practical needs, you will be ble to get by with some stock of common Spanish words and phrases, t is advisable also to have some understanding of the parts of speech nd their various forms as well as of the manner in which Spanish entences are constructed. In the following pages we have attempted ɔ present the "highlights" of Spanish grammar very concisely, so as ɔ enable you to understand the how and why of the phrases in this ook. This survey is of necessity brief, but the main facts for your aily needs have been covered.

1. THE ARTICLE

1.1. The definite article in Spanish has the following forms:

	Singular	Plural
Masculine	**el** (the)	**los** (the)
Feminine	**la** (the)	**las** (the)

1.2. Contractions of the masculine singular definite article are ɔrmed with the prepositions *a* and *de* : *al* (*a* + *el*) *hombre* (to the ıan) *del* (*de* + *el*) *hombre* (of the man).

1.3. The definite article in Spanish is used more often than in nglish.

1.4. The forms of the indefinite article in Spanish are:

	Singular	Plural
Masculine	**un** (a or an)	**unos** (some)
Feminine	**una** (a or an)	**unas** (some)

1.5. The indefinite article is not used in Spanish so often as in nglish.

1.6. Both the definite and indefinite articles agree in gender and ımber with the noun they modify.

1.7. The neuter article *lo* is used with participles and adjectives, as ▸ *dicho* (what has been said), *lo útil* (that which is useful).

2. THE NOUN

2.1. All nouns in Spanish are either masculine or feminine. Nouns ıding in *-o* are generally masculine; those ending in *-a* (except *-ma* and -*ta*), -*dad*, -*tad*, -*tud*, -*ión*, *umbre*, -*ez*, and *ie* are generally feminin[e]

2.2. The plural of nouns of both genders ending in an unstresse[d] vowel is formed by adding -*s* and of nouns ending in a consonant [or] a stressed vowel by adding -*es*: *el caballo* (the horse), *los caballos* (t[he] horses); *la yegua* (the mare), *las yeguas* (the mares); *la flor* (the flowe[r]) *las flores* (the flowers); *el rubí* (the ruby), *los rubíes* (the rubies).

2.3. In Spanish, possession is always expressed by the prepositi[on] *de* preceding the noun which designates the possessor: *el libro* [de] *Jorge* (George's book).

2.4. If the object (direct or indirect) denotes a person, it is precede[d] by the preposition *a*, which is then called **the personal a**. Compa[re] the following examples: *Espero a mi tía* (I wait for my aunt); *Bus[co] mi abrigo* (I am looking for my overcoat). This personal *a* is omitt[ed] when the object denoting a person is not identified: *Llame un polic[ía]* (Call a [= any] policeman).

2.5. Spanish speakers use a great number of diminutives (whi[ch] express smallness or affection) and augmentatives (which usua[lly] express large size or awkwardness), especially in colloquial spee[ch] These diminutives and augmentatives make the speech more color[ful] and add various connotations to the basic meanings of the words fro[m] which they are derived. One whose native tongue is not Spanish h[as] to be careful in the use of these forms because he may use a diminuti[ve] or augmentative formed with a certain suffix which has a basic co[n]notation but which in certain forms may have additional connotatio[ns] Examples: *pan* (bread), *panecito* (roll); *Ana* (Anna), *Anita* (Ann[ie]) *mano* (hand), *manecita* (pretty little hand); *pueblo* (town), *puebleci[to]* (tiny town); *libro* (book), *librito* (booklet), *librote* (large old boo[k]) *hombre* (man), *hombrón* (big man).

3. THE ADJECTIVE

3.1. There are two classes of adjectives in Spanish:

a) Those which end in -*o* in the m(asculine) s(ingular) and ha[ve] four forms (one for the m. s. in -*o*, one for the f(eminine) s. in -*a*, o[ne] for the m. pl(ural) in -*os*, and one for the f. pl. in -*as*): *el cua[rto] pequeño* (the small room), *los cuartos pequeños* (the small room[s]) *la casa pequeña* (the small house), *las casas pequeñas* (the sm[all] houses).

b) Those which end in -*e* or any vowel other than -*o* or in a co[n]sonant have only two forms, one for the singular and one for [the] plural of both genders: *el cuarto grande* (the large room), *la casa grande* (the large house); *los cuartos grandes* (the large rooms), *las casas grandes* (the large rooms).

3.2. The adjective agrees in gender and number with the noun it modifies. An adjective which modifies two or more nouns is always used in its masculine plural form if at least one noun is masculine: *Pepe y María son ricos* (Joe and Mary are wealthy).

3.3. The adjectives follow the same rules as the nouns for the formation of the plural.

3.4 In Spanish the usual position of the descriptive adjectives is after the noun they modify: *camino estrecho* (narrow road).

Limiting adjectives, such as demonstrative, interrogative, possessive and indefinite pronominal adjectives and numerals precede the noun they modify: *este libro* (this book); *cualquier libro* (any book [at all]); *el primer libro* (the first book).

Adjectives which express an inherent or characteristic quality of the modified noun or which are used with a figurative meaning also generally precede the noun they modify: *la blanca nieve* (the white snow); *la dura necesidad* (the hard necessity).

Some adjectives change their meaning according to their position before or after the noun, *un gran hombre* (a great man); *un hombre grande* (a big man).

A few adjectives, such as *bueno* (good), *malo* (bad), *pequeño* (small), as well as the ordinal numerals, may appear before or after the noun they modify without any basic change in their meaning.

3.5. The adjectives in Spanish, as in English, may be used as nouns: *el español* ([the] Spanish [language]); *los pobres y los ricos* (the poor and the rich).

3.6. The comparative is formed by placing *más* (more) before the adjective: *más hermoso* (more beautiful). The superlative is formed by adding the article to the comparative: *el (la) más hermoso(-a)* (the most beautiful).

Four adjectives have irregular comparative forms: *bueno* (good), *mejor* (better); *malo* (bad), *peor* (worse); *grande* (big), *mayor* or *más grande* (larger); *pequeño* (little), *menor* or *más pequeño* (smaller).

The comparison of superiority is expressed by *más* plus the adjective plus *que* and that of inferiority by *menos* plus the adjective plus *que*: *Ella es menos pobre que él* (She is less poor than he).

4. THE PRONOUN

4.1. The personal pronouns are:

Singular

Subject		Indirect object	Direct object	Prepositional (used after prepositions)	
yo	*I*	me	me	mí	*me*
tú (fam.)	*you*	te	te	ti	*you*
él	*he*	le	le, lo	él	*him*
ella	*she*	le	la	ella	*her*
usted	*you*	le	le, lo (m.), la (f.)	usted	*you*
él, ella	*it*	le	lo (m.), la (f.)	él, ella, ello	*it*

Plural

nosotros,-as	*we*	nos	nos	nosotros,-as	*us*
vosotros,-as (f.)	*you*	os	os	vosotros,-as	*you*
ellos	*they*	les	los	ellos	*them*
ellas	*they*	les	las	ellas	*them*
ustedes	*you*	les	los (m.), las (f.)	ustedes	*you*

The object pronouns are placed before the verb. Only in the case of an infinitive, an imperative or a gerund, are they placed after the verb and attached to it: *El me la* pagó* (He paid it to me); *Páguemela* (Pay it to me).

The indirect object must precede the direct object when a verb governs two object pronouns.

When both the direct and indirect object pronouns are in the third person, *se* is used for the indirect objects *le* and *les*: *Se lo doy* (I give it to him [her, them, you sing. and pl.]).

For emphasis and to avoid ambiguity, the prepositional pronouns are used in addition to the object pronouns: *El se la* pagó a usted* (He paid it to you); *Páguesela** (Pay it to her).

When the pronouns *mí, ti, sí* are governed by the preposition *con* (with), they form one word consisting of *con*, the pronoun and the particle *-go*: *conmigo* (with me), *contigo* (with you), *consigo* (with him, her, it, them).

4.2. Reflexive pronouns. The pronouns of the first, second an

---

* La in all these cases refers to *la cuenta* (bill).

hird persons have a reflexive meaning when they refer to the same
>erson as the subject:

(Yo) me equivoco	I am mistaken
(Tú) te equivocas	You are mistaken
(El) se equivoca	He is mistaken
(Nosotros) nos equivocamos	We are mistaken
(Vosotros) os equivócais	You are mistaken
(Ellos) se equivocan	They are mistaken

Usted and *ustedes* (polite forms of you) are also replaced by *se* in
he reflexive form: *Se equivoca(n) usted(es)* (you are mistaken).

4.3. The possessive adjectives are:

SHORT FORMS		LONG FORMS		*English*
(used before a noun)		*(used after a noun)*		*equivalents*
Singular	**Plural**	**Singular**	**Plural**	
ni	*mis*	*mio, -a*	*mios, -as*	my
u	*tus*	*tuyo, -a*	*tuyos, -as*	your
u	*sus*	*suyo, -a*	*suyos, -as*	his, her, its,
				your, their
uestro, -a	*nuestros, -as*	*nuestro, -a*	*nuestros, -as*	our
uestro, -a	*vuestros, -as*	*vuestro, -a*	*vuestros, -as*	your

The forms of the possessive pronouns in Spanish are identical with
he long forms of the possessive adjectives, but they are preceded by
he definite article: *el mío* (m. s.); *los míos* (m. pl.); *la mía* (f. s.); *las
nías* (f. pl.) (mine). They agree in gender and number with the noun
or which they stand.

The relative possessive adjective is *cuyo (-a)* which agrees in gender
nd number with the noun that follows it: *El viejo cuya casa compré
stá aquí* (The old man whose house I bought is here).

4.4. The interrogative pronouns are:

¿Quién? (who? whom?), of both genders, refers to persons only.

¿Qué? (what)), used with things and in many other cases.

¿Cuál? (which, which one?), used to select one from a large group
f persons or things.

Only *quién* and *cuál* have plural forms. They are *quiénes* and
uáles.

4.5. The demonstrative pronouns and adjectives. There is no dif-
erence in form between the demonstrative pronouns *éste, ésta* (this
ne); *éstos, éstas* (these ones); *ése, ésa* (that one); *ésos, ésas* (those ones);
quél, aquélla (that one) ; and *aquéllos, aquéllas* (those ones) and the
orresponding demonstrative adjectives *este, esta* (this); *estos, estas*
these); *esos, esas* (those); *aquel, aquella* (that); and *aquellos, aquellas*
those). The only difference between the two groups is that the pro-

nouns have a written accent on the stressed syllable while the adjec
tives are written without any accent. The demonstrative pronoun
stand by themselves, but the demonstrative adjectives precede the
nouns which they limit and modify. Examples: Adjective: *Este baúl e
de Ricardo* (This trunk is Richard's). Pronoun: *Este es mi baúl* (Thi
is my trunk).

The *este*-forms indicate an object which is near the person who
speaks; the *ese*-forms an object near the person addressed; and the
aquel-forms an object which is removed from both the speaker and
the person addressed.

In addition to the demonstrative pronouns, which have correspond
ing forms used as demonstrative adjectives, there are the neuter pro
nouns *esto, eso,* and *aquello* which have no written accent and ar
used when the thing for which they stand is a statement, idea of
something indefinite or unknown: *Esto es muy bueno* (This is very
good); *¡Eso es!* (That's it!).

4.6.a. The most common **indefinite pronouns** in Spanish are:

Alguien (someone, somebody, anyone, anybody), which refers to
persons only.

Algun(o), -a, -os, -as (someone, -body; anyone, -body) which refers to
persons or things.

Cualquiera (any one), which refers to persons only.

Nadie (no one, nobody, none, no), which refers to persons only.

Ningun(o), -a, -os, -as (no one, nobody, none, no), which refers to
persons or things.

Otro, -a (another, other), *otros, -as* (others), which refer to person
or things.

4.6.b. The most common **indefinite adjectives** in Spanish are:

1. Those that have four forms:

alguno, -a, -os, -as	some, any, a few
(alguno, -a que otro, -a	some . . . or other)
mucho, -a, -os, -as	much, many
ninguno, -a, (-os, -as)	not any, no
otro, -a, -os, -as	another, other
poco, -a, -os, -as	little, few
tanto, -a, -os, -as	as much, as many
todo, -a, -os, -as	all, every

2. Those that have only one form: *cada* (each), *los (las) dem*
(the rest [of]).

3. Those that have two forms: *ambos, ambas* (both), *cualquier*
cualesquiera (any [one] at all).

4.7. Relative pronouns. *Que* (who, whom, that, which) is the most common of the relative pronouns. It is used either as a subject or the direct object of a verb: *El libro que me dió usted es muy interesante* (The book [which] you gave me is very interesting); *Me gusta el libro que me dió usted* (I like the book [which] you gave me). Note in the above sentence that the word "which" or "that" (*que*), which may be and is often omitted in English, can *never* be omitted in Spanish.

Quien (who, whom) is used instead of *que* after prepositions and to introduce clauses which are not necessary to complete a sentence: *El niño de quien hablé está aquí* (The child of whom I spoke is here).

El que, la que, los que, las que; el cual, la cual, los cuales, las cuales may be used instead of *que* or *quien* to avoid ambiguity: *El perro de mi amiga, el cual desaparece a menudo, no está aquí ahora* (My girl friend's dog, which disappears often, is not here now).

Lo que (that which, what, which) is used as a relative pronoun which refers to a fact, an event, or an idea rather than to a person or a thing.

5. THE NUMERALS

5.1. The cardinal numbers are listed on page 20. They are all invariable, except *uno* (-*a*) and the compounds of *ciento* (a hundred), as *doscientos, -as* (two hundred), etc.

Uno drops the -*o* and *ciento* its final syllable -*to* when they immediately precede a noun.

5.2. The ordinal numbers are inflected exactly as adjectives. *Primero* and *tercero* drop the final -*o* when they precede a noun: *el tercer tomo* (the third volume).

6. THE PREPOSITION

6.1. The use of the prepositions is one of the most difficult things to master in learning a foreign language because prepositional usage is largely idiomatic. You should form the habit of observing and learning, through repetition and practice, the prepositional usages which differ from English as you encounter them.

The most common prepositions in Spanish are: *a* (to [direction]), *ante, antes de* (before [time]), *bajo* (under), *con* (with), *contra* (against), *de* (from), *delante de* (before [place]), *desde* (since), *después de* (after [time]), *detrás de* (behind [place]), *durante* (during), *en* (in, on), *entre* (between), *hacia* (toward [direction]), *hasta* (until), *para* (for [purpose, aim]), *por* (through, for [means, reason]), *según* (according to), *sin* (without), *sobre* (on, over), *tras* (after).

7. THE ADVERB

7.1. In Spanish, most of the adverbs of manner are formed by adding the suffix *-mente* to the singular feminine forms of adjectives:

rápido,-a	quick	*rápidamente*	quickly
fácil	easy	*fácilmente*	easily

7.2. In a series of adverbs in *-mente,* the suffix *-mente* is omitted from all except the last.

7.3. The comparative of adverbs is formed by placing *más* before the adverb; and the superlative by placing *lo más* before it.

Four very common adverbs have irregular comparatives: *bien* (well), *mejor* (better); *mal* (badly), *peor* (worse); *mucho* (much), *más* (more), *poco* (little), *menos* (less).

7.4. *Donde* is used as both interrogative and affirmative "where". In writing, the interrogative *dónde* takes an accent.

8. THE CONJUNCTION

8.1. Coordinating conjunctions join sentences, clauses, phrases, and words of equal rank. The most common ones in Spanish are: *y* (and), *o* (or), *pero, mas* (but); and the correlatives: *o . . . o* (either . . . or), *ni . . . ni* (neither . . . nor).

When *y* occurs before a word beginning with *i* or *hi,* it changes to *e,* and *o* before *o* or *ho* changes to *u*.

8.2. Subordinating conjunctions introduce dependent clauses. The most common ones are: *a fin de que* (in order to), *aunque* (although), *como* (as), *conque* (so that, so then), *con tal que* (provided that), *cuando* (when), *mientras que* (while), *para (que)* (in order to), *porque* (because), *puesto que* (since), *que* (that), *si* (if).

9. THE INTERJECTION

9.1. Some of the most common interjections in Spanish, and their approximate English meanings, are: *¡ay!* (ouch!, ah!, alas!), *¡ah!* (ah!), *¡bah!* (pshaw!), *¡hola!* (hello!), *¡viva!* (hurrah!), *¡caramba!* (confound it!).

9.2. Exclamative phrases are used as interjections:

¡Qué bonita! (How pretty!)	*¡Qué lástima!* (What a pity!)
¡Qué hermosa! (How beautiful!)	*¡No importa!* (Never mind!)

10. THE VERB

10.1. In English the form of the verb changes according to the subject. We say: I am, you are, he is, etc. In most cases, however, the English verb changes only in the third person singular in the present. Since most of the possible forms are identical, we are not especially conscious of the problem of verb endings. On the other hand, the Spanish verb has a large number of endings which differ according to subject, tense, and mood. The best way to learn the verb forms properly is in the context in which they are used.

There are three conjugations in Spanish and they are indicated by the ending of the infinitive:

1st CONJUGATION	2nd CONJUGATION	3rd CONJUGATION
dese-ar	**com-er**	**part-ir**
(to wish)	(to eat)	(to leave; to divide)

The stem of a verb is what is left after striking off the ending of the infinitive. The endings of the different moods, tenses, and persons are added to these stems.

10.2 INDICATIVE

Present

The Spanish *deseo* corresponds to the English "I wish," "I am wishing," "I do wish."

	First Conjugation	Second Conjugation	Third Conjugation
yo	dese-*o*	com-*o*	part-*o*
	(*I wish*)	(*I eat*)	(*I leave*)
tú	dese-*as*	com-*es*	part-*es*
usted (él, ella)	dese-*a*	com-*e*	part-*e*
nos	dese-*amos*	com-*emos*	part-*imos*
vos	dese-*áis*	com-*éis*	part-*is*
ustedes ellos, ellas	dese-*an*	com-*en*	part-*en*

The pronouns (*yo*, etc.) may be omitted in Spanish because the endings themselves indicate the subject (see 4.1).

The present indicative of regular verbs is formed by taking the stem of the verb and adding to it the endings which are printed in italics to help the student distinguish them.

Imperfect

(I wished, was wishing, used to wish, eat, leave, etc.)

dese-*aba*	com-*ía*	part-*ía*
dese-*abas*	com-*ías*	part-*ías*
dese-*aba*	com-*ía*	part-*ía*
dese-*ábamos*	com-*íamos*	part-*íamos*
dese-*abais*	com-*íais*	part-*íais*
dese-*aban*	com-*ían*	part-*ían*

Note that the second and third conjugations have identical endings for the imperfect.

Future

(I shall or will wish, eat, leave, etc.)

dese-*aré*	com-*eré*	part-*iré*
dese-*arás*	com-*erás*	part-*irás*
dese-*ará*	com-*erá*	part-*irá*
dese-*aremos*	com-*eremos*	part-*iremos*
dese-*aréis*	com-*eréis*	part-*iréis*
dese-*arán*	com-*erán*	part-*irán*

Preterit

dese-*é*	com-*í*	part-*í*
(I wished)	*(I ate)*	*(I left)*
dese-*aste*	com-*iste*	part-*iste*
dese-*ó*	com-*ió*	part-*ió*
dese-*amos*	com-*imos*	part-*imos*
dese-*asteis*	com-*isteis*	part-*isteis*
dese-*aron*	com-*ieron*	part-*ieron*

Conditional

(I should or would wish, eat, leave, etc.)

dese-*aría*	com-*ería*	part-*iría*
dese-*arías*	com-*erías*	part-*irías*
dese-*aría*	com-*ería*	part-*iría*
dese-*aríamos*	com-*eríamos*	part-*iríamos*
dese-*aríais*	com-*eríais*	part-*iríais*
dese-*arían*	com-*erían*	part-*irían*

COMPOUND TENSES

All compound tenses of both the indicative and the subjunctive are formed by the proper tense of the auxiliary verb *haber* plus the past participle.

Perfect

(Formed by the present of *haber* plus the past participle.)

he	dese-*ado*	he	com-*ido*	he	part-*ido*
has	dese-*ado*	has	com-*ido*	has	part-*ido*
ha	dese-*ado*	ha	com-*ido*	ha	part-*ido*
hemos	dese-*ado*	hemos	com-*ido*	hemos	part-*ido*
habéis	dese-*ado*	habéis	com-*ido*	habéis	part-*ido*
han	dese-*ado*	han	com-*ido*	han	part-*ido*

Pluperfect

(Formed by the imperfect of *haber* plus the past participle.)

había	deseado	había	comido	había	partido
habías	deseado	habías	comido	habías	partido
había	deseado	había	comido	había	partido
habíamos	deseado	habíamos	comido	habíamos	partido
habías	deseado	habíais	comido	habías	partido
habían	deseado	habían	comido	habían	partido

FUTURE PERFECT AND CONDITIONAL PERFECT

The future perfect is formed by the future of *haber* and the past participle of the verb, and the conditional perfect by the conditional of *haber* and the past participle.

Future Perfect	**Conditional Perfect**
(I shall have wished, eaten, left, etc.)	*(I should have wished, eaten, left, etc.)*

habré		habría	
habrás		habrías	
habrá	dese-ado	habría	dese-ado
habremos	com-ido	habríamos	com-ido
habréis	part-ido	habríais	part-ido
habrán		habrían	

10.3 THE SUBJUNCTIVE

The subjunctive in Spanish is used in subordinate clauses in which action is presented as a possibility and not as a fact, and after imper-

The subjunctive in Spanish is used in dependent clauses in which action is presented as a possibility and not a a fact, and after impersonal expressions introduced by *que* (that). Examples: *Creo que él lo haga* (I think that he may (will) do it); *Esperan que ella vuelva mañana* (They hope that she may (will) return tomorrow); *Es necesario que yo salga en seguida* (It is necessary for me to leave at once).

Note that in the first example the present subjunctive is used for both present and future time. The word "que" must never be omitted even when its corresponding word "that" in English is omitted.

When *creer* and other verbs of similar meaning in the main clause express certainty, the indicative is used in the dependent clause; when they express doubt or possibility, the subjunctive is used. Examples: *Creo que ellos son buenos* (I believe they are good); *Creo que ellos sean buenos* (I think that they may (will) be good).

When the verb of the main clause expresses desire, command, fear, wonder and similar emotions, the subjunctive is used in the dependent clause. Examples: *Ella quiere que usted compre eso* (She wants you to buy that); *Yo no quiero hacerlo pero él quiere que yo lo haga* (I don't want to do it, but he wants me to do it).

Note that when the subject is the same for both the main and the dependent verbs, the infinitive is used, as in English, but when the subject is different, the subjunctive is used in a dependent clause.

The tenses of the subjunctive are the present, the imperfect, the perfect and the pluperfect.

Present Subjunctive

dese-*e*	com-*a*	part-*a*
dese-*es*	com-*as*	part-*as*
dese-*e*	com-*a*	part-*a*
dese-*emos*	com-*amos*	part-*amos*
dese-*éis*	com-*áis*	part-*áis*
dese-*en*	com-*an*	part-*an*

Imperfect Subjunctive

The imperfect subjunctive has two forms, the *"ra"* form and the *"se"* form. The two forms have the same meaning. They may be used indiscriminately.

The Ra-Subjunctive

dese-*ara*	com-*iera*	part-*iera*
dese-*aras*	com-*ieras*	part-*ieras*
dese-*ara*	com-*iera*	part-*iera*
dese-*áramos*	com-*iéramos*	part-*iéramos*
dese-*arais*	com-*ierais*	part-*ierais*
dese-*aran*	com-*ieran*	part-*ieran*

The Se-Subjunctive

dese-*ase*	com-*iese*	part-*iese*
dese-*ases*	com-*ieses*	part-*ieses*
dese-*ase*	com-*iese*	part-*iese*
dese-*ásemos*	com-*iésemos*	part-*iésemos*
dese-*aseis*	com-*ieseis*	part-*ieseis*
dese-*asen*	com-*iesen*	part-*iesen*

The perfect and pluperfect subjunctives are formed by the present and imperfect subjunctives, respectively, of *haber* plus the past participle of the verb.

10.4 THE IMPERATIVE

The true imperative is used only in the familiar form of affirmative commands: *come* (eat [singular]), *comed* (eat [plural; very seldom used]).

The third person of the present subjunctive is used for the polite imperative: *coma* (eat). This is the form of the imperative used under normal circumstances and corresponds to the *usted*-form of the indicative and the subjunctive.

10.5 THE PARTICIPLES

The gerund or present participle is invariable in gender and number. It is used most frequently in connection with the verb *estar* to form the progressive tenses, and it expresses an action that continues or is continued:

Estoy hablando	**Estaremos comiendo**	**¿Está lloviendo?**
I am speaking	We shall be eating	Is it raining?

The past participle is formed by adding -*ado* to the stem of the verbs of the first conjugation and -*ido* to those of the second and third conjugations:

dese-ado (wished)   **com-ido** (eaten)   **part-ido** (left)

There is a small number of verbs which have irregular past participles.

10.6. The two Spanish verbs *ser* and *estar* corresponding to the English "to be" are included among the irregular verbs of the list. *Ser* is used with predicate adjectives to denote an inherent quality. *Estar* is used to denote a temporary quality or position.

10.7. The following pages list the most common irregular verbs in Spanish in the basic tenses and moods. The forms printed in bold face are irregular, and those in light face are regular.

IRREGULAR

INFINITIVE & PARTICIPLES	INDICATIVE			
	PRESENT	IMPERFECT	PRETERIT	FUTURE
andar, *to walk* andando andado	ando andas anda andamos andáis andan	andaba andabas andaba andábamos andabais andaban	**anduve anduviste anduvo anduvimos anduvisteis anduvieron**	andaré andarás andará andaremos andaréis andarán
caber, *to fit into* cabiendo cabido	**quepo** cabes cabe cabemos cabéis caben	cabía cabías cabía cabíamos cabíais cabían	**cupe cupiste cupo cupimos cupisteis cupieron**	**cabré cabrás cabrá cabremos cabréis cabrán**
caer, to fall **cayendo caído**	caigo caes cae caemos caéis caen	caía caías caía caíamos caíais caían	**caí caíste** cayó **caimos caísteis cayeron**	caeré caerás caerá caeremos caeréis caerán
dar, to give dando dado	**doy** das da damos dais dan	daba dabas daba dábamos dabais daban	**di diste dió dimos disteis dieron**	daré darás dará daremos daréis darán
decir, to say, tell **diciendo dicho**	**digo dices dice decimos decís dicen**	decía decías decía decíamos decíais decían	dije dijiste dijo dijimos dijisteis dijeron	**diré dirás dirá diremos diréis dirán**
estar, to be estando estado	estoy estás está estamos estáis están	estaba estabas estaba estábamos estabais estaban	**estuve estuviste estuvo estuvimos estuvisteis estuvieron**	estaré estarás estará estaremos estaréis estarán
haber, to have habiendo habido	he has ha hemos habéis han	había habías había habíamos habíais habían	**hube hubiste hubo hubimos hubisteis hubieron**	**habré habrás habrá habremos habréis habrán**

VERBS

CONDITIONAL	IMPERATIVE	SUBJUNCTIVE		
		PRESENT	IMPERFECT 1	IMPERFECT 2
andaría	anda	ande	anduviese	anduviera
andarías	andad	andes	anduvieses	anduvieras
andaría		ande	anduviese	anduviera
andaríamos		andemos	anduviésemos	anduviéramos
andaríais		andéis	anduvieseis	anduvierais
andarían		anden	anduviesen	anduvieran
cabría	cabe	**quepa**	cupiese	cupiera
cabrías	cabed	**quepas**	cupieses	cupieras
cabría		**quepa**	cupiese	cupiera
cabríamos		**quepamos**	cupiésemos	cupiéramos
cabríais		**quepáis**	cupieseis	cupierais
cabrían		**quepan**	cupiesen	cupieran
caería	cae	caiga	cayese	cayera
caerías	caed	caigas	cayeses	cayeras
caería		caiga	cayese	cayera
caeríamos		caigamos	cayésemos	cayéramos
caeríais		caigáis	cayeseis	cayerais
caerían		caigan	cayesen	cayeran
daría	da	dé	diese	diera
darías	dad	des	dieses	dieras
daría		dé	diese	diera
daríamos		demos	diésemos	diéramos
daríais		deis	dieseis	dierais
darían		den	diesen	dieran
diría	di	diga	dijese	dijera
dirías	decid	digas	dijeses	dijeras
diría		diga	dijese	dijera
diríamos		digamos	dijésemos	dijéramos
diríais		digáis	dijeseis	dijerais
dirían		digan	dijesen	dijeran
estaría	**está**	esté	estuviese	estuviera
estarías	estad	estés	estuvieses	estuvieras
estaría		esté	estuviese	estuviera
estaríamos		estemos	estuviésemos	estuviéramos
estaríais		estéis	estuvieseis	estuvierais
estarían		estén	estuviesen	estuvieran
habría	he	haya	hubiese	hubiera
habrías	habed	hayas	hubieses	hubieras
habría		haya	hubiese	hubiera
habríamos		hayamos	hubiésemos	hubiéramos
habríais		hayáis	hubieseis	hubierais
habrían		hayan	hubiesen	hubieran

INFINITIVE & PARTICIPLES	INDICATIVE			
	PRESENT	IMPERFECT	PRETERIT	FUTURE
hacer, *to make, do* **haciendo hecho**	hago haces hace hacemos hacéis hacen	hacía hacías hacía hacíamos hacíais hacían	hice hiciste hizo hicimos hicisteis hicieron	haré harás hará haremos haréis harán
ir, *to go* **yendo ido**	voy vas va vamos vais van	iba ibas iba íbamos ibais iban	fui fuiste fue fuimos fuisteis fueron	iré irás irá iremos iréis irán
oír, *to hear* **oyendo oído**	oigo oyes oye oímos oís oyen	oía oías oía oíamos oíais oían	oí oíste oyó oímos oísteis oyeron	oiré oirás oirá oiremos oiréis oirán
poder, *to be able* **pudiendo podido**	puedo puedes puede podemos podéis pueden	podía podías podía podíamos podíais podían	pude pudiste pudo pudimos pudisteis pudieron	podré podrás podrá podremos podréis podrán
poner, *to put* **poniendo puesto**	pongo pones pone ponemos ponéis ponen	ponía ponías ponía poníamos poníais ponían	puse pusiste puso pusimos pusisteis pusieron	pondré pondrás pondrá pondremos pondréis pondrán
querer, *to want* queriendo querido	quiero quieres quiere queremos queréis quieren	quería querías quería queríamos queríais querían	quise quisiste quiso quisimos quisisteis quisieron	querré querrás querrá querremos querréis querrán
saber, *to know* sabiendo sabido	sé sabes sabe sabemos sabéis saben	sabía sabías sabía sabíamos sabíais sabían	supe supiste supo supimos supisteis supieron	sabré sabrás sabrá sabremos sabréis sabrán

| CONDITIONAL | IMPERATIVE | SUBJUNCTIVE | | |
		PRESENT	IMPERFECT 1	IMPERFECT 2
haría	haz	haga	hiciese	hiciera
harías	haced	hagas	hicieses	hicieras
haría		haga	hiciese	hiciera
haríamos		hagamos	hiciésemos	hiciéramos
haríais		hagáis	hicieseis	hicierais
harían		hagan	hiciesen	hicieran
iría	ve	vaya	fuese	fuera
irías	id	vayas	fueses	fueras
iría		vaya	fuese	fuera
iríamos		vayamos	fuésemos	fuéramos
iríais		vayáis	fueseis	fuerais
irían		vayan	fuesen	fueran
oiría	oye	oiga	oyese	oyera
oirías	oíd	oigas	oyeses	oyeras
oiría		oiga	oyese	oyera
oiríamos		oigamos	oyésemos	oyéramos
oiríais		oigáis	oyeseis	oyerais
oirían		oigan	oyesen	oyeran
podría		pueda	pudiese	pudiera
podrías		puedas	pudieses	pudieras
podría		pueda	pudiese	pudiera
podríamos		podamos	pudiésemos	pudiéramos
podríais		podáis	pudieseis	pudierais
podrían		puedan	pudiesen	pudieran
pondría	pon	ponga	pusiese	pusiera
pondrías	poned	pongas	pusieses	pusieras
pondría		ponga	pusiese	pusiera
pondríamos		pongamos	pusiésemos	pusiéramos
pondríais		pongáis	pusieseis	pusierais
pondrían		pongan	pusiesen	pusieran
querría	quiere	quiera	quisiese	quisiera
querrías	quered	quieras	quisieses	quisieras
querría		quiera	quisiese	quisiera
querríamos		queramos	quisiésemos	quisiéramos
querríais		queráis	quisieseis	quisierais
querrían		quieran	quisiesen	quisieran
sabría	sabe	sepa	supiese	supiera
sabrías	sabed	sepas	supieses	supieras
sabría		sepa	supiese	supiera
sabríamos		sepamos	supiésemos	supiéramos
sabríais		sepáis	supieseis	supierais
sabrían		sepan	supiesen	supieran

INFINITIVE & PARTICIPLES	INDICATIVE			
	PRESENT	IMPERFECT	PRETERIT	FUTURE
salir, *to go out* saliendo salido	salgo sales sale salimos salís salen	salía salías salía salíamos salíais salían	salí saliste salió salimos salisteis salieron	saldré saldrás saldrá saldremos saldréis saldrán
ser, *to be* siendo sido	soy eres es somos sois son	era eras era éramos erais eran	fui fuiste fue fuimos fuisteis fueron	seré serás será seremos seréis serán
tener, *to have* teniendo tenido	tengo tienes tiene tenemos tenéis tienen	tenía tenías tenía teníamos teníais tenían	tuve tuviste tuvo tuvimos tuvisteis tuvieron	tendré tendrás tendrá tendremos tendréis tendrán
traducir, *to translate* traduciendo traducido	traduzco traduces traduce traducimos traducís traducen	traducía traducías traducía traducíamos traducíais traducían	**traduje** **tradujiste** **tradujo** **tradujimos** **tradujisteis** **tradujeron**	traduciré traducirás traducirá traduciremos traduciréis traducirán
traer, *to bring* **trayendo** traído	traigo traes trae traemos traéis traen	traía traías traía traíamos traíais traían	**traje** **trajiste** **trajo** **trajimos** **trajisteis** **trajeron**	traeré traerás traerá traeremos traeréis traerán
valer, *to be worth* valiendo valido	valgo vales vale valemos valéis valen	valía valías valía valíamos valíais valían	valí valiste valió valimos valisteis valieron	valdré valdrás valdrá valdremos valdréis valdrán
venir, *to come* viniendo venido	vengo vienes viene venimos venís vienen	venía venías venía veníamos veníais venían	vine viniste vino vinimos vinisteis vinieron	vendré vendrás vendrá vendremos vendréis vendrán
ver, *to see* viendo visto	veo ves ve vemos veis ven	veía veías veía veíamos veíais veían	ví viste vió vimos visteis vieron	veré verás verá veremos veréis verán

CONDITIONAL	IMPERATIVE	SUBJUNCTIVE		
		PRESENT	**IMPERFECT 1**	**IMPERFECT 2**
saldría	**sal**	**salga**	saliese	saliera
saldrías	**salid**	**salgas**	salieses	salieras
saldría		**salga**	saliese	saliera
saldríamos		**salgamos**	saliésemos	saliéramos
saldríais		**salgáis**	salieseis	salierais
saldrían		**salgan**	saliesen	salieran
sería	**sé**	**sea**	**fuese**	**fuera**
serías	sed	**seas**	**fueses**	**fueras**
sería		**sea**	**fuese**	**fuera**
seríamos		**seamos**	**fuésemos**	**fuéramos**
seríais		**seáis**	**fueseis**	**fuerais**
serían		**sean**	**fuesen**	**fueran**
tendría	**ten**	**tenga**	**tuviese**	**tuviera**
tendrías	**tened**	**tengas**	**tuvieses**	**tuvieras**
tendría		**tenga**	**tuviese**	**tuviera**
tendríamos		**tengamos**	**tuviésemos**	**tuviéramos**
tendríais		**tengáis**	**tuvieseis**	**tuvierais**
tendrían		**tengan**	**tuviesen**	**tuvieran**
traduciría	traduce	**traduzca**	**tradujese**	**tradujera**
traducirías	traducid	**traduzcas**	**tradujeses**	**tradujeras**
traduciría		**traduzca**	**tradujese**	**tradujera**
traduciríamos		**traduzcamos**	**tradujésemos**	**tradujéramos**
traduciríais		**traduzcáis**	**tradujeseis**	**tradujerais**
traducirían		**traduzcan**	**tradujesen**	**tradujeran**
traería	trae	**traiga**	**trajese**	**trajera**
traerías	traed	**traigas**	**trajeses**	**trajeras**
traería		**traiga**	**trajese**	**trajera**
traeríamos		**traigamos**	**trajésemos**	**trajéramos**
traeríais		**traigáis**	**trajeseis**	**trajerais**
traerían		**traigan**	**trajesen**	**trajeran**
valdría	**val(e)**	**valga**	valiese	valiera
valdrías	**valed**	**valgas**	valieses	valieras
valdría		**valga**	valiese	valiera
valdríamos		**valgamos**	valiésemos	valiéramos
valdríais		**valgáis**	valieseis	valierais
valdrían		**valgan**	valiesen	valieran
vendría	**ven**	**venga**	**viniese**	**viniera**
vendrías	**venid**	**vengas**	**vinieses**	**vinieras**
vendría		**venga**	**viniese**	**viniera**
vendríamos		**vengamos**	**viniésemos**	**viniéramos**
vendríais		**vengáis**	**vinieseis**	**vinierais**
vendrían		**vengan**	**viniesen**	**vinieran**
vería	ve	**vea**	**viese**	**viera**
verías	ved	**veas**	**vieses**	**vieras**
vería		**vea**	**viese**	**viera**
veríamos		**veamos**	**viésemos**	**viéramos**
veríais		**veáis**	**vieseis**	**vierais**
verían		**vean**	**viesen**	**vieran**

USEFUL INFORMATION FOR MOTORISTS

NARROW ROAD

DETOUR AT M

NARROW BRIDGE

PAVEMENT ENDS

STOP

SLOW

SHARP TURN

R.R. CROSSING

CURVE

ROAD CROSSING

ROAD JUNCTION

MEN AT WORK

Road Signs

SPANISH-ENGLISH DICTIONARY

A

a at, to
abajo below
abierto,-a open
abogado *m.* lawyer
abrigo *m.* overcoat
abril *m.* April
abrir to open
absolutamente absolutely
abuela *f.* grandmother
abuelo *m.* grandfather
acaso perhaps
accidental accidental
accidente *m.* accident
acción *f.* action
aceituna *f.* olive
acelerador *m.* accelerator
acera *f.* sidewalk
acerca de concerning,
   with regard to
acompañar to accompany
acordar to remind
acordarse to remember
acostar to lay down,
   to put to bed
acostarse to go to bed,
   to lie down
actor *m.* actor
actriz *f.* actress
acuático,-a aquatic
acumulador *m.* battery
adelantado,-a advanced, fast
adelante forward
adentro inside
admirable wonderful,
   admirable
adorno *m.* ornament,
   trimming
aduana *f.* custom-house

aeronáutico,-a aeronautic
aeroplano *m.* airplane
aeropuerto *m.* airport
afeitarse to shave
aficionado *m.* (fan of a sport)
agencia *f.* agency
agente *m.* agent
agosto *m.* August
agradable agreeable, pleasant
agricultura *f.* agriculture
agricultor *m.* farmer
agua *m.* water
   ... caliente hot water
   ... fría cold water
   ... helada ice water
aguardiente *m.* brandy
águila *m.* eagle
aguja *f.* needle
ahora now
   ... mismo right now,
   at once
aire *m.* air
ajo *m.* garlic
ajustar to adjust, to fit
al to the, at the, on the
alemán,-a German
alemania *f.* Germany
albaricoque *m.* apricot
alcachofa *f.* artichoke
alcalde *m.* mayor
alcoba *f.* bedroom
alcohol *m.* alcohol
alegrarse to be glad
alfombra *f.* rug
algo something, some
algodón *m.* cotton
alguien somebody
alguno,-a someone

alimento *m.* food
allí there
allá there, in that place
 por . . ., that way
almacén *m.* shop
almendra *f.* almond
almohada *f.* pillow
almorzar to have lunch
almuerzo *m.* lunch
alquilar to hire
alondra *f.* lark
alto loud, high, tall
alto stop (imp.)
amanecer *m.* daybreak
amapola *f.* poppy
amargo,-a bitter
amarillo,-a yellow
ambos,-as both
ambulancia *f.* ambulance
América del Sur *f.* South
 America
americano,-a American
amigo *m.* friend
amor *m.* love
amplio,-a wide
amueblado,-a furnished
ancho,-a broad, wide
andar to walk
angosto,-a narrow
animal *m.* animal
anoche last night
anochecer to become dark
ante, antes de before
anteayer day before yesterday
Antillas *f.* West Indies,
 Antilles
antiséptico,-a antiseptic
anual annual
anunciar to advertise,
 to announce
anuncio *m.* advertisement
año *m.* year
Año Nuevo *m.* New Year
apagar to put out, turn off
apenas scarcely
aperitivo *m.* aperitif
apetito *m.* appetite
apio *m.* celery
aplaudir to applaud

apostar to bet
apreciación *f.* appreciation
apreciar to appreciate
aprender to learn
apretado,-a tight
aprieto *m.* jam, tight spot
aprisa quick
apuesta *f.* bet
apurarse to hurry
apúrese hurry up (imp.)
aquí here
 por . . ., this way
arado *m.* plow
árbol *m.* tree
ardilla *f.* squirrel
armario *m.* closet, wardrobe
aromático,-a aromatic
arqueología *f.* archeology
arquitecto *m.* architect
arquitectura *f.* architecture
arranque automático
 self-starter
arrendar to rent, to lease
arriba above
arroz *m.* rice
arte *m.* art
artículos *m.* goods, articles
artificial artificial
artista *m.,f.* artist
artístico,-a artistic
asado,-a roasted, broiled
 bien . . . well done
asar to roast
ascender to rise, to climb
ascensor *m.* elevator
aseado,-a *m.* tidy
así so, thus
asiento *m.* seat
asistencia *f.* assistance,
 attendance
asistir to attend
aspirina *f.* aspirin
astringente *m.* astringent
asuntos *m.* affairs
asustarse to get frightened
atender to attend
atómico,-a atomic
atractivo,-a attractive
atrás backward, behind

atrasado,-a slow, backward
aún still, yet
aunque although
aurora *f.* dawn
auto *m.* automobile
autobús *m.* bus
automóvil *m.* automobile
autoridad *f.* authority
avellana *f.* hazelnut
avena *f.* oats
avenida *f.* avenue
aviación *f.* aviation
avión *m.* airplane, airliner
¡ay! alas!
ayuntamiento *m.* city hall
ayer yesterday
azúcar *m.* sugar
azucarero *m.* sugar bowl
azucena *f.* white lily
azul *m.* blue

B

bailar to dance
baile *m.* dance
  pista de . . . dance floor
bajar to go or come down, to get off, to get down
bajo,-a low, soft, under
balcón *m.* balcony
balde *m.* bucket
  de . . . free
  en . . . in vain
banco *m.* bank
banda *f.* band
bañarse to bathe oneself
baño *m.* bath
  cuarto de . . . bathroom
bañera *f.* bathtub
bar *m.* bar
barato,-a cheap
barco *m.* ship
barómetro *m.* barometer
basta that is enough
bastante enough, quite, sufficiently
barrer to sweep
batata *f.* sweet potato
baúl *m.* trunk
beber to drink

bebida *f.* drink
  . . . gaseosa soft drink
becerro *m.* calf
beisbol *m.* baseball
bermellón *m.* vermilion
bicicleta *f.* bicycle
bien well
  yo estoy . . . I am well
biftec *m.* beefsteak
billete *m.* ticket, paper money
biblioteca *f.* library
bien well
bisté *m.* steak
blanco,-a white
blando,-a soft
blusa *f.* blouse
bordado *m.* embroidery
bocina *f.* automobile horn
boleto *m.* ticket
bollo, *m.* rolls (bread)
bolsillo *m.* pocket
bolso,-a purse
bonito,-a pretty
bosque *m.* woods
bostezo *m.* yawn
botas *f., pl.* boots
botella *f.* bottle
botica *f.* drugstore
botón *m.* button
brazo *m.* arm
brisa *f.* breeze
buen good
bueno,-a good
  buena suerte good luck
  buenas noches good night
  buenas tardes good afternoon
  buenos días good morning
buey *m.* ox
bujía *f.* spark plug
burla *f.* mockery, jest
  de . . . for fun
burro *m.* donkey
buzón *m.* mailbox

C

caballero *m.* gentleman
caballo *m.* horse

cabina *f.* airplane cabin
cabeza *f.* head
cable *m.* cable
cablegrama *m.* cablegram
cabra *f.* goat
cacao *m.* cocoa
cada each
caer to fall
caerse to fall down
café *m.* coffee
   ... **con leche,** coffee with
    milk
cafetera *f.* coffee pot
caja *f.* box
cajero,-a cashier
calcetines *m., pl.* socks
calefacción *f.* heating
calendario *m.* calendar
caliente hot
calabaza *f.* pumpkin
calle *f.* street
calor *m.* warmth, heat
  tengo ... I am hot
calzado *m.* footwear
cama *f.* bed
cámara *f.* camera
camarera *f.* room maid
camarero,-a waiter, waitress
camarote *m.* cabin
camarón *f.* shrimp
cambiar to change
cambiarse to change (clothes)
cambio *m.* change, exchange
caminar to walk
camino *m.* road
camión *m.* truck, bus (Mex.)
camioneta station wagon
camisa *f.* shirt
camiseta *f.* undershirt
campo *m.* country, field
canario *m.* canary
canasta *f.* basket
canción *f.* song
cansado,-a tired
cansarse to get tired
cantar to sing
cantidad *f.* quantity
canto *m.* song
cara *f.* face

carbón *m.* carbon, coal
carácter *m.* character
carcajada *f.* burst of laughter
cárcel *f.* jail
¡caramba! *inter.* gracious!
   strange!
carnaval *m.* carnival
carne *m.* meat
   ... **de res** *f.* beef
carnero *m.* sheep, mutton
carnicería *f.* butcher shop
caro,-a expensive
carreras de caballos
   horseraces
carretera *f.* highway
carretero *m.* cart-driver
carro *m.* cart, car
carta *f.* letter
  papel de ... writing paper
cartera *f.* handbag, wallet
casa *f.* home, house
   ... **de huéspedes** boarding
    house
casi *adv.* almost
casino *m.* club
castaña *f.* chestnut
castaño *m.* chestnut tree,
   brown
catarro *m.* cold (illness)
catedral *f.* cathedral
católico,-a a catholic
catorce fourteen
cebada *f.* barley
cebolla *f.* onion
celebrar to celebrate,
   to approve
celebridad *f.* celebrity
celos *m.* jealousy
cena *f.* supper
cenar to dine, to have supper
centavo *m.* cent
centeno *m.* rye
centígrado centigrade
central central
céntrico,-a central
Centro América *f.* Central
   America
cepillarse to brush

cepillo *m.* brush
  ... de dientes toothbrush
cerca near
cerdo *m.* pig
cereal *m.* cereal
cereza *f.* cherry
cerilla *f.* match
cero *m.* zero
cerrado,-a closed
cerrar to close, shut
cerveza *f.* beer
chaleco *m.* vest
chanclos *m.* rubbers (shoes)
chaqueta *f.* coat, jacket
cheque *m.* check
  ... viajero travelers check
chicle *m.* chewing gum
chimenea *f.* chimney
chino,-a Chinese
chiquito,-a small, little
chiste *m.* joke
chistoso,-a funny
chocolate *m.* chocolate
chuleta *f.* chop
  ... de puerco pork chop
cielo *m.* sky
ciento hundred
  por ... per cent
cierto,-a certain, sure
  por ... incidentally
ciervo *m.* deer
cigarrillo *m.* cigarette
cigarro *m.* cigar
cinco *m.* five
cincuenta m. fifty
cine *m.* motion-picture
  theater
cinta *f.* ribbon
cintura *f.* waist, waistline
cinturón *m.* belt
circo de toros *m.* bullring
ciruela *f.* plum
cita *f.* appointment, date
ciudad *f.* city
claro clearly, pale, light
clase *f.* class, kind
  primera ... first class
  segunda ... second class
clavel *m.* carnation

clima *m.* climate
clínica *f.* clinic, doctor's office
club *m.* club
cobre *m.* copper
coche *m.* car
cocina *f.* kitchen
cocinar to cook
cocinera *f.* cook
coco *m.* cocoanut
coctel *m.* cocktail
codo *m.* elbow
coger to catch
col *f.* cabbage
colcha *f.* bedspread
colchón *m.* mattress
colegio *m.* school
coliflor *f.* cauliflower
colonia *f.* colony
color *m.* color
colorado,-a red
comedor *m.* dining room
comenzar to begin
comer to eat
comercial commercial
comerciante *m.* merchant
comida *f.* dinner, food
como as
¿cómo? how?
cómoda *f.* chest of drawers
cómodo,-a comfortable
compañía *f.* company
comparación *f.* comparison
componer to compose
  to repair
compostura f. repair
compra *f.* purchase
comprar to buy
  ¿dónde puedo ...? where
  can I buy?
comprender to understand
comprendido,-a understood
compromiso *m.* appointment,
  date
comúnmente commonly
con with
concierto m. concert
conductor *m.* driver,
  conductor
conejo *m.* rabbit

confeti *m.* confetti
conforme alike, suitable
  . . . a according to
congelado,-a frozen
conmigo with me
conocer to know (people,
  places), to be introduced to
conocimiento *m.* knowledge,
  bill of lading
conque so then, so that
constar to consist
construir to build,
  to construct
contado,-a rare
  al . . . (for) cash
contar to count
contento-a happy
contestar to answer
contra against
contraer to contract
contrario,-a contrary
  al . . . on the contrary
consistir to consist
consulta *f.* visit (doctor's),
  consultation
convencer to convince
conveniente convenient
conversación *f.* conversation
copia *f.* copy
corbata *f.* necktie
cordero *m.* lamb
cordial cordial
corrección *f.* correction
correcto,-a correct
corredor *m.* corridor, hall
correo *m.* mail
  . . . aéreo airmail
correspondencia *f.*
  correspondence
corriente *f.* current, draft
cortar to cut
cortés courteous
cortesía *f.* courtesy
cortina *f.* curtain
corto,-a short
  muy . . . too short
cosa *f.* thing
coser to sew
cosecha *f.* harvest

cosmético *m.* cosmetic
costa *f.* coast
costar to cost
costillas *f.* ribs
costura *f.* seam, sewing
cotización *f.* quotation
crecer to grow
crecimiento *m.* growth
credencial *f.* credential
crédito *m.* credit
  a . . . on credit
creer to believe, to think
  (opinion)
crema *f.* cream
crepé *m.* crepe
criada *f.* maid
criminal *m.* criminal
cristal *m.* crystal
crudo,-a raw
cuaderno *m.* notebook
cuadra *f.* block
cuadrado *m.* square
cuadro *m.* picture
cuál which
cuales which
cualesquiera whoever
cualquier any
cualquiera anyone, whatever
cuando when
cuánto how much, how many
cuarenta forty
cuaresma *f.* lent
cuarto *m.* quarter, fourth,
  room
cuatro four
cubano-a, Cuban
cubierta *f.* envelope
cubierto *m.* silverware
cubrir to cover
cucaracha *f.* cockroach
cuchara *f.* spoon
cucharada *f.* spoonful
cucharita *f.* teaspoon
cuchilla *f.* razor blade
cuchillo *m.* knife
cuello *m.* collar, neck
cuenta *f.* bill, restaurant
  check, account
cuento *m.* story

cuervo *m.* raven
cuidado caution
cuidar to take care of
¡cuidado! be careful!
cumpleaños *m.* birthday
cuñada *f.* sister-in-law
cuñado *m.* brother-in-law

D

dar to give
dátil *m.* date
de from, of
dé give (imp.)
debajo beneath, under
deber ought, should, must
debilidad *f.* weakness
decidir to decide
décimo,-a tenth
decir to say, to tell
decisión *f.* decision
declaración *f.* declaration
decorar to decorate
dedo *m.* finger
deducción *f.* deduction
defectivo,-a defective
defecto *m.* defect
defender to defend
dejar to leave, to allow, to let
del of the, from the, about the
delante before
delgado thin
delicioso,-a delicious
demasiado too much
démelo give it to me
dentista *m.,f.* dentist
dentro inside
   ... de within
departamento *m.* apartment,
   department
depositado deposited
depositar to deposit
derecha *f.* right
derecho straight, straight
   ahead
derretir to melt
desabrido,-a tasteless
desagradable disagreeable
desalquilado,-a free, unhired,
   unrented

desamueblado,-a unfurnished
desaparecer to disappear
desastroso,-a disastrous
desayuno *m.* breakfast
descansar to rest
descender to descend, to go
   down
descompuesto,-a out of order
descontar to discount
describiendo describing
describir to describe
descubrir to discover
descripción *f.* description
descriptivo,-a descriptive
descuento *m.* discount
desde from
desear to wish
desenvolver to unwrap
deseo *m.* desire
deshacerse to get rid of
desinfectante *m.* disinfectant
desobedecer to disobey
despacio slowly
despacho *m.* office, despatch,
   shipment
despedirse to take leave of
despertar to wake up
después after
desvestirse to undress
desvío *m.* detour
detener to detain
detestar to detest
detrás behind
devolver to return (a thing)
día *m.* day
diagnóstico *m.* diagnosis
diamante *m.* diamond
diario *m.* daily, journal
diccionario *m.* dictionary
diciembre *m.* December
diecinueve nineteen
dieciocho eighteen
dieciséis sixteen
diecisiete seventeen
diente *m.* tooth
diez ten
diferencia *f.* difference
diferente different
difícil difficult

dificultades *f.* troubles, difficulties

dígame tell me

digestible digestible

digestión *f.* digestion

digo I say, tell

dije I said, told

dinero *m.* money

Dios God

diplomacia *f.* diplomacy

diplomático,-a diplomat

dirección *f.* address, direction

directo,-a direct

directorio *m.* directory

disco *m.* phonograph record

discurso *m.* speech

discusión *f.* discussion

discutir to discuss, to argue

dispensar to excuse

dispénseme excuse me

distancia *f.* distance

distribución *f.* distribution

distribuir to distribute

dividir to divide

diversión *f.* entertainment

divertirse to have a good time

dividido divided

doble double

doce twelve

docena *f.* dozen

doctor,-a doctor

dólar *m.* dollar

doler to hurt

dolor *m.* ache

domingo *m.* Sunday

donde where

dormir to sleep

dormirse to go to sleep

dormitorio *m.* bedroom, dormitory

dos two

doy I give

duda *f.* doubt, uncertainty

dudar to doubt

dueño,-a owner

dulce sweet

durable durable

duradero,-a durable, lasting

durante during

durar to last

duro,-a tough, hard

E

¡Ea! Well!

echar to pour, to throw, to dump, to put out

edificio *m.* building

efectivo,-a effective

hacer . . . to cash

ejotes *m.* string beans

el the

él he

electricidad *f.* electricity

eléctrico,-a electric

elefante *m.* elephant

elegante elegant

elevado,-a high

elevador *m.* elevator

ella she

embarcar to sail, embark

emborracharse to get drunk

embrague *m.* clutch

emergencia *f.* emergency

en in, on, at

encaje *m.* lace

encerrar to lock in

encima above, overhead

. . . de on, upon

encender to light, to burn

. . . la luz to put on the light

encontrar to meet, to find, to encounter

encuentro *m.* encounter

enero *m.* January

enfermedad *f.* sickness

enfermarse to get sick

enfermo,-a sick

estoy . . . I am sick

enfriarse to get cold

enojado,-a angry

ensalada *f.* salad

enseñar to teach, to show

entender to understand

entendido understood

enterarse to find out

yo entiendo I understand

entonces then

entrar to enter, to go in, to come in
entre between, among
entrega f. delivery
entregar to deliver
entretener to entertain
entusiasmarse to get enthusiastic
entusiasmo enthusiasm
envío m. shipment
envolver to wrap
envuelto,-a wrapped
equipaje m. baggage
equivalente equivalent
equivocarse to make a mistake
era was, were, used to be, it was, it used to be
error m. error
es is, are, it is
escalera f. staircase, ladder
escalones stairs, steps
escribiendo writing
escritorio m. desk
escuela f. school
escultura f. sculpture
esencial essential
eso,-a that
espacioso,-a spacious, roomy
espalda f. back
España f. Spain
español,-a Spaniard, Spanish
espárragos m. asparagus
especial special
especialmente specially
esperado hoped, waited, expected
esperanza f. hope
esperar to hope, to wait, to expect
espinaca f. spinach
esposa f. wife
esposo m. husband
esponja f. sponge
esquina f. corner
esta f. this
ésta f. this one
está is, (you) are
  ¿cómo . . . usted? how are you?

establecer to establish
estación f. station, season
  . . . de gasolina gas station
estacionar to park
estadio m. stadium
estado m. state, been
Estados Unidos m. United States
estamos we are
estampilla f. stamp
están they are, you are
estaño m. tin
estar to be
estatua f. statue
este,-a this
este m. east
éste this one
estilo m. style
estómago m. stomach
estornudo m. sneeze
estos m. these
estoy I am
estrecho,-a tight, narrow
estudiante student
estúpido,-a stupid
estuve I was
evadir to evade, avoid
exactamente exactly
exacto,-a exact
exageración f. exaggeration
exagerar to exaggerate
examinar to examine
excavación f. excavation
excessivo,-a excessive
excepto except
excúseme excuse me
exhibición f. exhibition
exigir to demand
existencia f. existence
éxito m. success
experiencia f. experience
explicar to explain
exportar to export
expresar to express
exterior exterior, outside room
extranjero,-a foreign, foreigner
extraño,-a strange, foreign

F

fábrica *f.* factory
facial facial
fácil easy
facilidad *f.* facility, ease
facturar to check, to invoice
faja *f.* girdle
falda *f.* skirt
falta *f.* lack, want
faltar to lack, to miss
famoso,-a famous
fango *m.* mud
farmacia *f.* drugstore
familia *f.* family
favor *m.* favor
fealdad *f.* ugliness
fabrero *m.* February
fecha *f.* date
felicidad *f.* happiness
felicitar to congratulate
feo,-a ugly
ferrocarril *m.* railroad
fervor *m.* fervor, enthusiasm
festival *f.* festival
festividad *f.* festivity, feast
fieltro *m.* felt
fiesta *f.* feast
   día de . . . holiday
fiebre *f.* fever, temperature
filete *m.* cutlet
fin *m.* end, conclusion
   al . . . at last
   por . . . at last
   en . . . finally
finalmente finally
firma *f.* firm, concern
firmar to sign
flor *f.* flower
florista *m.,f.* florist
flotando floating
flotar to float
fluctuación fluctuation
fogón *m.* fireplace, stove
fonógrafo *m.* phonograph
formal formal
formar to form
fortuna *f.* fortune
fósforo *m.* match

foto *f.* photograph
fotografía *f.* photograph
fotografiar to photograph
fracasar to fail
fracaso *m.* failure
fracción *f.* fraction
frambuesa *f.* raspberry
francés,-sa French,
   Frenchman, Frenchwoman
Francia *f.* France
frecuentemente frequently
fregadero *m.* sink
freír to fry
frenos *m.* automobile brakes
frente in front, opposite
fresa *f.* strawberry
fresco *m.* cool, fresh
fríjoles *m.* beans
frío,-a cold
   tengo . . . I am cold
frito,-a fried
fruta *f.* fruit
fuente *f.* platter, tray,
   fountain
fuera without, outside
fuerte *m.* fort
fuí I was, I went
fumar to smoke
funeral *m.* funeral
futbol *m.* football (soccer)

G

gabardina *f.* gabardine,
   raincoat
galleta *f.* cracker, cookie
gallina *f.* hen
gallo *m.* cock
   pelea de gallos cock fight
gallera *f.* cock pit
ganado *m.* cattle
ganancia *f.* profit
ganso *m.* goose
ganas *f.* desire, yen
garage *m.* garage
gas *m.* gas
gasolina *f.* gasoline
gato *m.* cat
gaveta *f.* locker
generador *m.* generator

general *m.* general
generalmente generally, ordinarily
género m. material, gender
gente *f.* people
ginebra *f.* gin
girar to spin
giro *m.* draft
gloria *f.* glory
golondrina *f.* swallow
gobierno *m.* government
golf *m.* golf
goma *f.* rubber
gordo,-a fat
gorra *f.* cap
gozo *m.* joy
gracia *f.* grace, charm
gracias *f.* thank you, thanks
gracioso,-a graceful, amusing
grande large, big
grado *m.* degree
granja *f.* farm
grano *m.* grain
gratis gratis, free
grave grave, very ill
gris *m.* gray
gritar to shout, to scream
grito *m.* shout, scream
gruesa *f.* gross
guagua *f.* bus (Cuba)
guantes gloves
guapo,-a handsome
guías del viajero road map
guisado *m.* stew
guisantes *m.* peas
guitarra *f.* guitar
gustar to like
    si gusta if you please
gusto *m.* taste, pleasure

H

ha you have (he, she, it) has
haber to be
había there was, there were, was there?, were there? there used to be, did there used to be?
habichuelas *f.* beans

habitación *f.* room, chamber
habitantes inhabitants
habla (he, she) speaks (you) speak
hablado talked
hablar to speak
hacer to do
hacia toward
hacienda *f.* ranch, large farm
hambre *m.* hunger
    tengo . . . I am hungry
hasta up to, until
    . . . la vista, . . . luego until we meet again
hay there is, there are
    . . . que it is necessary
helada *f.* frost
helado *m.* ice cream
helar to freeze
hélice *f.* propeller
heno *m.* hay
hermana *f.* sister
hermano *m.* brother
hermoso,-a beautiful
hermosura *f.* beauty
hervir to boil
hielo *m.* ice
higo *m.* fig
hija *f.* daughter
hijo *m.* son
hilo *m.* thread
hipo *m.* hiccough
historia *f.* history
hogar *m.* home
hoja *f.* sheet, leaf
¡Hola! Hello!
hombre *m.* man
hombro *m.* shoulder
hora *f.* hour, time
honor *m.* honor
horario *m.* hour hand, timetable
horno *m.* oven
hortelano *m.* farmer, gardener
hospital *m.* hospital
hospitalidad *f.* hospitality
hoy today

hubo there was, there were, was there? were there?
huerta *f.* orchard
huevo *m.* egg
   ... duro hard boiled egg
   ... frito fried egg
   ... pasado por agua soft boiled egg
humor *m.* humor
húngaro,-a Hungarian
humedad *f.* humidity

I

iba (he, she, it) went, used to go, was going
idea *f.* idea
idioma *m.* language
iglesia *f.* church
ignorancia *f.* ignorance
ignorante ignorant
igual equal
ilegal illegal
ilustración *m.* illustration
imaginación *m.* imagination
imitación *f.* imitation
impaciencia *f.* impatience
impermeable *m.* raincoat, waterproof
importante important
importar to import
importe *m.* amount, value
imposibilidad *f.* impossibility
imposible impossible
imprimir to print
impuesto *m.* duty (tax)
incluír to include
incompetente incompetent
incorrecto,-a incorrect
independencia *f.* independence
indigestión *f.* indigestion
indispuesto,-a indisposed
indolente indolent
industrial industrial
infección *f.* infection
influencia *f.* influence
informar to inform

ingeniero *m.* engineer
Inglaterra *f.* England
inicial initial
inmenso,-a immense
inocular to inoculate
insecto *m.* insect
insignificante insignificant
instalar to install
instante *m.* instant
insultar to insult
insulto *m.* insult
inteligente intelligent
interior *m.* interior
internacional international
interrumpir to interrupt
íntimamente intimately
íntimo,-a intimate
itinerario *m.* timetable
introducción *f.* introduction
invierno *m.* winter
invitación *f.* invitation
invitado,-a a guest, visitor
invitar to invite
ir to go
irse to go away
italiano,-a Italian
itinerario *m.* itinerary
izquierda *f.* left

J

jardín *m.* garden
jarra *f.* pitcher
jabalí *m.* boar
jabón *m.* soap
jabonera *f.* soap dish
jamás never
jamón *m.* ham
jefe *m.* chief, boss
jornales wages
joven young
joyería *f.* jewelry store
judío,-a Jewish
juego *m.* game
   hacer ... to match
jueves *m.* Thursday
jugar to play (a game), to gamble
jugo *m.* juice
juguete *m.* toy

juicio *m.* judgment
julio *m.* July
junio *m.* June
junto near, close
juntos,-as together
justicia *f.* justice
justillo *m.* brassiere
justo-a just, fair
juventud *f.* youth

K

kilo *f.* kilo, kilogram

L

la the
lago *m.* lake
lágrima f. tear
lámpara *f.* lamp
lana *f.* wool
lancha *f.* launch, boat
lápiz *m.* pencil
largo,-a long
  muy ... too long
lastimarse to hurt oneself
lavandería *f.* laundry
lavarse to wash (oneself)
lavabo *m.* wash basin
lavar to wash
leal loyal
lección *f.* lesson
lechuga *f.* lettuce
leche *f.* milk
leer to read
legal legal
legumbre *f.* vegetable
lejos far
  ¿qué tan ... es? how far
    is it?
lengua *f.* tongue
lentejas *f.* lentils
león *m.* lion
leopardo *m.* leopard
letra *f.* letter
letrero *m.* sign
levantar to raise, to lift,
  pick up
  levantarse to get up
liar to tie

librería *f.* bookstore
libro *m.* book
liebre *f.* hare
lima *f.* lime
limón *m.* lemon
limonada *f.* lemonade
limpiar to clean
limpiavidrios *m.* windshield
  wiper
limpio-a clean
lino *m.* linen
lío *m.* a scrape, trouble
lirio *m.* lily
lista *f.* list
  ... de platos bill of fare
listo,-a ready
llama *f.* llama
llamar to call
llamarse to be called (name)
llanta *f.* tire
llave *f.* key
llegada *f.* arrival
llegar to arrive
  al ... upon arrival
llegué I arrived, got here,
  got there
llevar to wear, to carry, to take
  (someone or something
  some place)
llorar to cry
llover to rain
lluvia *f.* rain
lo *m.* it, him
lobo *m.* wolf
local local
loco,-a crazy
lodo *m.* mud
lotería *f.* lottery
lubricación *f.* lubrication
lubricante *m.* lubricant
lubricar to lubricate
luego later
  hasta ... so long
lugar *m.* place
lujo *m.* luxury
luna *f.* moon
lunes *m.* Monday
luz *f.* light

M

madera *f.* wood
madre *f.* mother
madrugada *f.* dawn
maestro,-a teacher
mal badly, ill
maleta *f.* suitcase
malo,-a bad
mamá *f.* mom, mama
mandado *m.* errand
mandar to send
manecillas hands (of a watch)
manejar to drive, to manage
manga *f.* sleeve
mano *f.* hand
mansión *f.* mansion
mantel *m.* tablecloth
mantequilla *f.* butter
manzana *f.* apple
mañana *f.* morning,
   tomorrow
   ... por la ... tomorrow
   morning
mapa *m.* map
máquina *f.* machine
   ... de escribir typewriter
maquinaria *f.* works,
   machinery
marcha *f.* march
   en ... it is starting
marearse to get seasick, airsick
mareo *m.* dizziness
marina *f.* navy
martes *m.* Tuesday
marzo *m.* March
más more
   ... que more than
masa *f.* bread, dough
matriculación *f.* registration
matricular to matriculate,
   to register
mayo *m.* May
mayor main, major, eldest
mazorca *f.* ear of corn
mí me, myself
mecánico,-a mechanic
medianoche *f.* midnight
mediante by means of

medias stockings
medicinal medicinal
médico *m.* doctor
medicina *f.* medicine
medio means, middle, half
   por ... de by means of
mediodía *m.* midday, noon
medir to measure
mejor better
mejorarse to get better
melocotón *m.* peach
melón *m.* melon
memoria *f.* memory
menos but, except, less
   al ... at least
mentir to lie
mentira *f.* lie
menú *m.* menu
menudo,-a small, little,
   minute
   a ... often
mercado *m.* market place
mercancía *f.* merchandise
mermelada *f.* marmalade
mes *m.* month
   por ... by the month
mesa *f.* table
metal *m.* metal
mexicano,-a Mexican
mi my
mídaselo try it on (imp.)
miedo *m.* fear
miel de abejas *f.* honey
miércoles *m.* Wednesday
mil thousand
mina *f.* mine
mineral *m.* mineral
minutero *m.* minute hand
minuto *m.* minute
   espere un ... wait a minute
mío,-a mine
mire look (imp.)
mismo,-a same
mis my
mitad *f.* half
moda *f.* fashion, style
moderno,-a modern
modista *f.* dressmaker
modo *m.* manner

molestar to bother
momento *m.* moment
moneda *f.* money, currency
monetario,-a monetary
mono *m.* monkey
morder to bite
moreno,-a brunette
mosaico *m.* mosaic, tile
mosco *m.* fly
mostaza *f.* mustard
mostrar to show
motor *m.* motor
motorista *m.,f.* motorist
moviendo moving
muchacha *f.* girl
muchacho *m.* boy
mucho,-a much
muchos,-as many
mudar to move
mueble *m.* furniture
muelle *m.* pier
muestra *f.* sample
mujer *f.* woman
mula *f.* mule
mundo *m.* world
mural *m.* mural
museo *m.* museum
música *f.* music
muy very
    . . . bien very well

N

nabo *m.* turnip
nacionalidad *f.* nationality
nacer to be born
nacimiento *m.* birth
nación *f.* nation
nacional national
nada nothing
nadar to swim
nadie nobody
naranja *f.* orange
    jugo de . . . *m.* orange juice
natilla *f.* custard
nativo,-a *f.* native
natural natural
naturalmente naturally
Navidad *f.* Christmas

necesario,-a necessary
necesidad *f.* necessity
necesitar to need
negativo negative
negligente negligent
negocio *m.* business
negro,-a black
nena *f.* baby girl
nene *m.* baby boy
nervioso,-a nervous
nevar to snow
ni . . . ni neither . . . nor
nieta *f.* granddaughter
nieto *m.* grandson
nieve *f.* snow
ninguno no one
niña *f.* girl
niñez *f.* childhood
niño,-a child
no no
noble noble
noche *f.* evening, night
    esta . . . tonight
Noche Buena *f.* Christmas
    Eve
nombre *m.* name
norte *m.* north
Norte América *f.* North
    America
norte americano,-a North
    American
nos us, ourselves
nosotros,-as we, us
nota *f.* note
notar to note, to notice
notario *m.* notary public
noticiario *m.* newsreel
noticias *f.* news
noventa ninety
noviembre *m.* November
nublado,-a cloudy
nuestro,-a our, ours
nueve nine
nuevo,-a new
nuez *f.* nut
número *m.* number
numeroso,-a numerous
nunca never

O

o either, or
obtener to obtain
ocasión f. occasion
occidente m. west, occident
oculista m.,f. oculist
ocupación f. occupation
ocupado,-a busy
ocho eight
ochenta eighty
octubre m. October
ocupar to occupy
ocurrir to occur
odiar to hate
odio m. hatred
ofender to offend
ofendido,-a offended
ofensivo,-a offensive
oficial official
oficina f. office
ofrecer to offer
oiga listen, hear (imp.)
oír to hear
ola f. wave
olfato m. smell
olivo m. olive-tree
olvidar to forget
once eleven
onza f. ounce
ópera f. opera
operador m. operator
operación f. operation
opinión f. opinion
órdenes orders
    a sus . . . at your service
ordinario,-a ordinary
oreja f. ear
oriente east, orient
original original
orquesta f. orchestra
orquídea f. orchid
oro m. gold
oscuro,-a dark
oso m. bear
ostra f. oyster
otoño m. autumn
otro,-a other
    uno u . . . one or the other

otros,-as others, other
oveja f. sheep
oye hear, listen (imp.)

P

paciencia f. patience
paciente patient
padre m. father
padres m. parents
pagar to pay
pago m. payment
país m. country
pagué I paid
paja f. straw
pájaro m. bird
pala f. shovel
palabra f. word
palacio m. palace
palma f. palm tree
palmeras f. palm trees
paloma f. dove
pan m. bread
pantalla f. movie screen,
    lamp shade
pantalones m. trousers
paño m. cloth
pañuelo m. handkerchief
papa f. potato
papel m. paper
papelería f. stationery store
paquete m. package
par m. pair, couple
para for, to
parabrisa m. windshield
paraguas m. umbrella
pararse to stand up, to stop
pardo brown
pare stop (imp.)
parecer to appear, seem
parecerse to resemble
pared f. wall
pargo m. red snapper
parientes m. relatives
parque m. park
parqueadero m. parking
parrilla f. grill
pasa f. raisin

pasado,-a past
... **mañana** day after tomorrow
pasaje *m.* ticket
pasar to pass
Pascua *f.* Easter
pasear to take a walk, a ride
dar un **paseo** to go for a walk, ride
pasta *f.* paste
pastel *m.* pie
pastor *m.* shepherd
patio *m.* inner court
patriótico,-a patriotic
patrón *m.* boss, pattern
pato *m.* duck
pavimento *m.* pavement
pavo *m.* turkey
pedir to order, to ask
peine *m.* comb
película *f.* film
peligro *m.* danger
peligroso,-a dangerous
pelo *m.* hair
penicilina penicillin
pensamiento *m.* thought, pansy
pensar to think
pensión *f.* pension, boarding house
peón *m.* peasant
peor worse
pepino *m.* cucumber
pequeño,-a small
muy ... ,-a too small
pera *f.* pear
perder to lose
perdiz *f.* partridge
perezoso,-a lazy
perfecto-a perfect
perfume *m.* perfume
periódico *m.* newspaper
permanente permanent, permanent wave
permítame allow me
permitido,-a permitted
permitir to allow
pero but
perro *m.* dog

personal personal
personalmente personally, in person
persuadir to persuade
pesar to weigh
pesarse to weigh yourself
pescado *m.* fish
pescar to fish
peso *m.* weight, peso
petróleo *m.* petroleum, crude oil
picante hot, spicy, piquant
pie *m.* foot
piedra *f.* stone, jewel
piel *f.* leather, hide
pierna *f.* leg
pieza *f.* room, piece, part
píldora *f.* pill
piloto *m.* pilot
pimienta *f.* pepper
pintar to paint
pintura *f.* painting
piña *f.* pineapple
pipa *f.* pipe
piscina *f.* swimming pool
piso *m.* floor
... **bajo** ground floor
placer *m.* pleasure
plan *m.* plan
planchar to iron
planta *m.* plant
plátano *m.* banana
plato *m.* dish, plate
playa *f.* beach
plaza *f.* square, market
pluma *f.* pen
pobre poor
poco,-a little
poder to be able
policía *m.* policeman
política *f.* politics
pollo *m.* chicken
polvo *m.* powder
poner to put, to set
ponerse to put on
ponqué *m.* cake
popular popular
populoso,-a densely populated
por by, for, through

porque because
   por qué why
portezuela *f.* car door
posible possible
posiblemente possibly
posición *f.* position
positivo,-a positive
postal *f.* postal
postre *m.* dessert
postrero,-a last
practicar to practice
práctico,-a practical
precio *m.* price
precioso,-a precious
predilecto,-a preferred,
   favorite
preferir to prefer
pregunta *f.* question
preguntar to ask
premio *m.* prize
preocupada,-a worried
preocupar to worry
preparar to prepare
presentar to present,
   to introduce
presente *m.* present
prestar to lend
primavera *f.* Spring
primero,-a first
primo,-a cousin
principal principal
prisa *f.* haste
   de ... quickly, fast
   dése ... hurry (imp.)
probablemente probably
probar to taste, to prove,
   to test
proceder to proceed
producir to produce
producto *m.* product
profesión *f.* profession
programa *m.* program
progresar to progress
progreso *m.* progress
prohibir to prohibit
   prohibida la entrada keep
   out
prometer to promise

pronto soon, fast
   de ... suddenly
pronunciación *f.*
   pronunciation
pronunciar to pronounce
propina *f.* tip
propio,-a proper, own
protección *f.* protection
protestante Protestant
protestar to protest
provincia *f.* province
provincial provincial
próximo,-a next
prueba *f.* proof
publicación *f.* publication
público,-a public
pueblo *m.* town
puente *m.* bridge
puerco *m.* pork, pig
puerta *f.* door
pues since, for
pulsera *f.* bracelet
   reloj de ... wristwatch
pulso *m.* pulse
puerto *m.* port
punto *m.* point, dot
   en ... exactly
puntual punctual
puño *m.* cuff, fist
puro *m.* cigar

Q

que that, which
qué what, which
   ... es eso? what is that
quebrar to break
quedarse to stay, to remain
quejido *m.* groan
querer to want, to love
queso *m.* cheese
quién who
quienquiera whoever
quince fifteen
quizá perhaps

R

rábano *m.* radish
racial racial
radiador *m.* radiator

radio radio
rancho *m.* ranch
rápidamente rapidly
rápido,-a rapid
rascarse to scratch
rata *f.* rat
ratón *m.* mouse
raro,-a rare, odd
  rara vez seldom
rayón *m.* rayon
razón *f.* reason
realizar to make, perform,
  realize
recibidor *m.* living room
receta *f.* prescription
recibir to receive
recibo *m.* receipt
reciente recent
reclamación *m.* complaint
reclamar to complain
recomendación *f.*
  recommendation
recomendar to recommend
reconocer to recognize
recordar to remember
recreación *f.* recreation
recuerdo *m.* souvenir
reducir to reduce
refajo *m.* slip
reflector *m.* reflector
refrescar to refresh
refrigeración *f.* refrigeration
refrigeradora *f.* refrigerator
región *f.* region
registración *f.* registration
registrar to register
regresar to return
regularidad *f.* regularity
reírse to laugh
relación *f.* relation
relativo,-a relative
relámpago *m.* lightning
reloj *m.* watch
relojería *f.* watch shop
relojero *m.* watchmaker
remendar to mend
remolacha *f.* beet
renta *f.* rent, income
reparar to repair

repente, de suddenly
repetir to repeat
repollo *m.* cabbage
requerir to require
resbalarse to slip, to slide
resfriado *m.* cold (illness)
resfriarse to catch cold
residencial residential
respetable respectable
responsable responsible
restaurante *m.* restaurant
resto *m.* rest
  el . . . the rest
restricción *f.* restriction
reunión *f.* reunion
revolver to mix
revuelto scrambled
ridículo,-a ridiculous
río *m.* river
risa *f.* laughter
robar to steal, to rob
robo *m.* theft, robbery
robustez *m.* robustness
rogar to beg
rojo,-a red
rollo *m.* roll film
romántico,-a romantic
romper to tear, to break
ron *m.* rum
roncar to snore
ropa *f.* clothes
  . . . interior underwear
rosa *f.* rose
rosario *m.* rosary
rosbif *m.* roast beef
rubio,-a blond
ruborizarse to blush
rueda *f.* wheel
rumba *f.* rumba
rumor *m.* rumor
rural *m.* rural
ruso Russian
ruta *f.* route

S

sábado *m.* Saturday
sábana *f.* sheet
saber to know
sacacorchos *m.* corkscrew

saco *m.* coat
sal *f.* salt
sala *f.* living room
salado,-a salty
salida *f.* departure, exit
salario *m.* salary
salir to leave
salsa *f.* sauce, dressing
saltar to jump
salud *f.* health
saludar to greet
saludo *m.* greeting
salvar to save
sandía *f.* watermelon
sandwich *m.* sandwich
sarape *m.* Mexican blanket
sardina *f.* sardine
sastre *m.* tailor
sastrería *f.* tailor shop
satisfacer to satisfy
secarse to dry (yourself)
sección *f.* section
secretario,-a secretary
sed thirst
    tengo ... I am thirsty
seda *f.* silk
sedativo *m.* sedative
seis six
según according to
segundo,-a second
seguro,-a safe
seguro *m.* insurance
selección *f.* selection
seleccionar to select, choose
sello *m.* stamp, seal
semana *f.* week
    por ... by the week
    ... Santa Holy Week
    esta ... this week
sembrar to sow
sentar to sit, to fit
señalar to show, point
señor *m.* Mr., sir, gentleman
señorita *f.* Miss, young girl
sentarse to sit down
sentir to feel, to be sorry
septiembre *m.* September
séptimo,-a seventh
ser to be

serpiente *f.* serpent
servicio *m.* service
servilleta *f.* napkin
servir to serve
seta *f.* mushroom
si if
sí yes
siempre always
    ... que whenever
siento I feel
    lo ... I am sorry
siete seven
siglo *m.* century
silencio silence
silla *f.* chair
sillón *m.* armchair
simpático,-a charming,
    sympathetic
simple single, simple
simplicidad *f.* simplicity
sin without
sinceridad *f.* sincerity
síntomas *m.* symptoms
sistema *m.* system
sitio *m.* place, location
situación *f.* situation
situar to situate
sobre on, upon
sobre *m.* envelope
sobrina *f.* niece
sobrino *m.* nephew
sociable sociable
social social
sociedad *f.* society
sofá *m.* sofa
sofocante suffocating
sol *m.* sun
solo,-a alone
sollozo *m.* sob
solución *f.* solution
sombra *f.* shade
sombrero *m.* hat
sombrerería *f.* hat store
soñar to dream
sonreírse to smile
sopa *f.* soup
sorprender to surprise
soso,-a insipid, tasteless
suave soft

subir to enter, to go up
suburbio *m.* suburb
sucesivamente successively
sucio,-a dirty
sucursal *f.* branch
sudar to perspire
suegra *f.* mother-in-law
suegro *m.* father-in-law
suela *f.* sole
suelo *m.* ground
sueño *m.* dream
suerte *f.* luck
suéter *m.* sweater
suficiente sufficient, enough
supuesto assumed, supposed
   por . . . of course
sur *m.* south
Sur América *f.* South America
suspiro *m.* sigh
suyo yours, his, hers

T

tabaco *m.* tobacco
tabla *f.* board
tacto *m.* touch
tacón *m.* heel
talla *f.* size
talle *m.* waist
talón *m.* baggage check
tal vez maybe
también also
tampoco neither
tango *m.* tango
tanque *m.* tank
tanto,-a as much, so much
tantos,-as as many, so many
taquilla *f.* box office
tarde *f.* afternoon, late
   más . . . later
tarea *f.* task
tarjeta *f.* card
taxi *m.* taxicab
taza *f.* cup
té *m.* tea
teatro *m.* theater
tela *f.* fabric
telefonear to telephone
teléfono *m.* telephone

telegrafista *m.f.* telegraph
   operator
telegrama *m.* telegram
televisión *f.* television
temer to fear
temperatura *f.* temperature
temprano early
tenedor *m.* fork
tener to have
tenis *m.* tennis
tercero,-a third
terciopelo *m.* velvet
terminado,-a finished
terminar to finish
termómetro *m.* thermometer
ternera *f.* veal, calf
terrible terrible
testigo *m.* witness
tía *f.* aunt
tiempo *m.* time
   a . . . in time
tienda *f.* store
tierno,-a tender
tierra *f.* earth
tigre *m.* tiger
tijeras *f.* scissors
timbre *m.* electric bell
tinta *f.* ink
tintero *m.* inkstand
tinto *m.* red (wine)
tintorería *f.* dyer's or
   cleaner's shop
tío *m.* uncle
típico,-a typical
tipo *m.* type
toalla *f.* towel
tobillo *m.* ankle
tocador *m.* dresser, boudoir
tocante a concerning
tocar to play (instrument), to
   ring, to knock on the door
tocino *m.* bacon
todavía yet
todo everything
todos,-as all
tomate *m.* tomato
tomar to take, to drink
toreo *m.* bullfight
torero,-a bullfighter

tormenta *f.* storm
toro *m.* bull
torrente *m.* torrent
tortilla *f.* omelet
tos *f.* cough
tostada *f.* toast
tostar to toast
total *m.* total
trabajador *m.* workman
trabajar to work
trabajo *m.* work
traducir to translate
traer to bring, to wear
tráfico *m.* traffic
traje *m.* suit
tranquilo,-a tranquil, peaceful
transacción *f.* transaction
transparente transparent
transportar to transport
tras behind
tratar (de) to try (to)
treinta thirty
tren *m.* train
tres three
trigo *m.* wheat
trimestre *m.* quarterly
   por . . . every three months
triste sad
trivial trivial
tropical tropical
trópico *m.* tropics
trucha *f.* trout
trueno *m.* thunder
turista *m.* tourist

U

últimamente lately
último,-a last
ultramarino,-a ultramarine
uno one
un *m.*; **una** *f.* a, an
universal universal
universidad *f.* university
uno,-a one
unos *m.*, **unas** *f.* some
urgente urgent
usar to use

usted (usually abbreviated V., Vd., U., Ud.) you
ustedes you (pl.)
utilidad *f.* utility
uva *f.* grape

V

vaca *f.* cow
vacación *f.* vacation
vacilar to hesitate
vainilla *f.* vanilla
vajilla dinnerware
valor *m.* value, bravery
vals *m.* waltz
vámonos let's go
vapor *m.* steamship, steam
varios,-as several
vaselina *f.* vaseline
vaso *m.* drinking glass
veces *f.* occasions, times
vecino,-a neighbor
vehículo *m.* vehicle
veinte twenty
vejez *f.* old age
velocidad *f.* speed
vender to sell
venir to come
ventana *f.* window
ventilador *m.* ventilator, electric fan
ventilar to ventilate
ventisca *f.* blizzard
ventura *f.* happiness, luck, chance
   por . . . by chance
ver to see
verano *m.* Summer
veras reality, truth
   ¿de . . . ? really?
verdad *f.* truth
   ¿no es . . . ? Is it not so?
   ¿es . . . ? Is it so?
   en . . . indeed
verde green
verse to appear, to look
vertical vertical
vestíbulo *m.* lobby
vestido *m.* dress
vestir to dress

vestirse to dress (yourself)
vez *f.* time
  una . . . once
  tal . . . maybe
vía, una one way
viajar to travel
viaje *m.* trip
viajero-a traveler
vida *f.* life
viejo,-a old
vienés,-a Viennese
viento *m.* wind
viernes *m.* Friday
vinagre *m.* vinegar
vino *m.* wine
violeta *f.* violet
visita *f.* visit
visitar to visit
víspera *f.* eve
vista *f.* view, sight
  con . . . a overlooking
vistoso,-a showy, beautiful
vital vital
vitamina *f.* vitamin

¡Viva! Hurrah!
vitrina *f.* shop window
vivir to live
vocabulario *m.* vocabulary
volar to fly
volcar to turn over, overturn
voluntad *f.* will
volver to return
volverse to become
vuelo *m.* flight

Y

y and
ya already
yegua *f.* mare
yerno *m.* son-in-law
yo I
yodo *m.* iodine

Z

zanahoria *f.* carrot
zapatería *f.* shoe store
zapatilla *f.* slipper
zapato *m.* shoe
zorro *m.* fox

ENGLISH-SPANISH DICTIONARY

A

a, an un, una
able, to be poder
above encima, arriba
absolutely absolutamente
accelerator acelerador *m.*
accident accidente *m.*
accidental accidental
accompany, to acompañar
according to según,
    conforme a
ache dolor *m.*
action acción *f.*
actor actor *m.*
actress actriz *f.*
address dirección *f.*
adjust, to ajustar
admirable admirable
adolescence adolescencia *f.*
advanced adelantado,-a
advertise, to anunciar
advertisement anuncio
aeronautic aeronáutico,-a
after después
against contra
age, old vejez *f.*
agency agencia *f.*
agent agente *m.*
agreeable agradable
agriculture agricultura *f.*
air aire *m.*
airmail correo aéreo
airplane aeroplano *m.*
    avión *m.*
airport aeropuerto *m.*
    puerto aéreo, *m.*
alas! ¡ay!
alcohol alcohol *m.*
alike conforme

all, todo,-a; todos,-as
allow me permítame
alone solo,-a
allow, to permitir, dejar
almond almendra *f.*
almost casi
already ya
also tambien
although aunque
always siempre
ambulance ambulancia *f.*
American americano,-a
among entre
amount importe *m.*
amusing gracioso
and y
angry enojado,-a
animal animal *m.*
ankle tobillo *m.*
announce, to anunciar
annual anual
any cuálquier
anyone cualquiera
answer, to contestar
answered contestado,-a
antenna antena *f.*
antiseptic antiséptico,-a
apartment departamento *m.*
aperitif aperitivo *m.*
appear, to parecer, verse
appetite apetito *m.*
applaud aplaudir
apple manzana *f.*
appointment cita *f.*;
    compromiso *m.*
appreciate, to apreciar
appreciation apreciación *f.*
apricot albaricoque *m.*
April abril *m.*
approve, to aprobar, celebrar

aquatic acuático,-a
archeology arqueología f.
architect arquitecto m.
architecture arquitectura
argue, to discutir
arm brazo m.
armchair sillón m.
aromatic aromático,-a
arrival llegada f.
arrive, to llegar
art arte m.
article artículo m.
artificial artificial
artist artista m., f.
artistic artístico,-a
artichoke alcachofa f.
as como
ash ceniza f.
ask, to preguntar, pedir
asparagus espárrago m.
aspirin aspirina f.
assistance asistencia f.
astringent astringente m.
at a, en
atomic atómico,-a
at once ahora
attend, to asistir, atender
attendance asistencia f.
attractive atractivo,-a
August agosto m.
aunt tía
authority autoridad f.
automobile automóvil,
    auto m.
autumn otoño m.
avenue avenida f.
aviation aviación f.
avoid, to evadir
away, to go irse

B

back espalda f.
backward atrasado,-a, atrás
bacon tocino m.
bad malo,-a
badly mal
baggage equipaje m.
baggage check talón m.
balcony balcón m.

banana plátano m.
band banda f.
bank banco m.
bar bar m.
barley cebada f.
barometer barómetro m.
baseball beisbol m.
basket canasta f.
bath baño m.
bathe (yourself), to bañarse
bathroom cuarto de baño
bathtub bañera f.
battery acumulador m.
be, to ser, estar, haber
be careful! ¡cuidado!
beach playa f.
beans fríjoles m.
bear oso m.
beautiful hermoso,-a
beauty hermosura
beauty parlor salón de belleza
become, to volverse
bed cama f.
bedroom dormitorio, m. alcoba f.
bedspread colcha f.
beef carne de res f.
beefsteak biftec m.
been estado
beer cerveza f.
beet remolacha f.
before delante, ante,
    antes de
beg, to rogar
begin, to comenzar
begun comenzado,-a
behind detrás, atrás
believe, I yo creo
believe, to creer
bell (electric) timbre m.
below abajo, debajo
belt cinturón m.
beneath debajo
bet apuesta f.
bet, to apostar
better mejor
better, to get mejorarse
between entre
bicycle bicicleta f.
big grande

bill cuenta *f.*
bird pájaro *m.*
birth nacimiento *m.*
bite, to morder
bitter amargo,-a
black negro,-a
blizzard ventisca *f.*
block cuadra *f.*
blond rubio,-a
blouse blusa *f.*
blue azul *m.*
blush, to ruborizarse
boarding house casa de
 huéspedes, pensión *f.*
boat barco *m.*
boil, to hervir
book libro *m.*
bookstore librería *f.*
boot bota *f.*
born, to be nacer
boss jefe, patrón *m.*
both ambos,-as
bother, to molestar
bottle botella *f.*
bought comprado,-a
box caja *f.*
box office taquilla *f.*
boy niño, muchacho *m.*
bracelet pulsera *f.*
brakes (automobile) frenos
brandy aguardiente *m.*
bravery valor *m.*
bread pan *m.*
break, to romper, quebrar
breakfast desayuno *m.*
breeze brisa *f.*
bridge puente *m.*
bring, to traer
broad ancho,-a
broiled asado,-a
brother hermano
brother-in-law cuñado *m.*
brown pardo
brunette moreno,-a
brush cepillo *m.*
brush, to cepillar
bucket balde *m.*
bud capullo *m.*
build, to construir

building edificio *m.*
bull toro *m.*
bullfight toreo *m.*
bullfighter torero,-a
bullring circo de toros *m.*
burn, to encender
bus autobús *m.*; camión *m.*
 (Mex.); guagua *f.* (Cub.)
business negocio *m.*
busy ocupado,-a
but pero, sino
butcher shop carnicería *f.*
butter mantequilla *f.*
button botón *m.*
buy, to comprar
 ... where can I ¿dónde
 puedo comprar?
by por
by means of mediante

C

cabbage col *f.* repollo *m.*
cabin camarote *m.*
cabin, airplane cabina *f.*
cablegram cablegrama *m.*
cake ponqué *m.*
calendar calendario *m.*
calf becerro *m.*
call, to llamar
called, to be (name) llamarse
camera cámara *f.*
canary canario *m.*
cap gorra *f.*
car carro *m.*
carbon carbón *m.*
card tarjeta *f.*
cardinal cardinal
care, to take cuidar
carnation clavel *m.*
carnival carnaval *m.*
carrot zanahoria *f.*
carry, to llevar
cart driver carretero *m.*
cashier cajero,-a
cat gato,-a
catch, to coger
cathedral catedral *f.*
Catholic católico,-a
cattle ganado *m.*

cauliflower coliflor *f.*
caution cuidado
celebrate, to celebrar
celebrity celebridad *f.*
celery apio *m.*
cent centavo *m.*
centigrade centígrado
central central
centuple céntuplo
century siglo *m.*
cereal cereal *m.*
certain cierto,-a
chair silla *f.*
chance, by por ventura
change cambio *m.*
change, to cambiar
character carácter *m.*
charm gracia *f.*
charming simpático,-a
cheap barato,-a
check cheque *m.*
check, restaurant cuenta *f.*
check, to facturar
cheese queso *m.*
cherry cereza *f.*
chest of drawers cómoda *f.*
chestnut castaña *f.*
chewing gum chicle *m.*
chicken pollo *m.*
child niño,-a
childhood niñez *f.*
Chinese chino,-a
chocolate chocolate *m.*
choose, to seleccionar
chops chuletas *f.pl.*
Christmas Navidad *f.*
Christmas Eve Noche
  Buena *f.*
church iglesia *f.*
cigar cigarro puro *m.*
cigarette cigarrillo *m.*
circular circular
city ciudad *f.*
city hall ayuntamiento *m.*
class clase *f.*
clean limpio,-a
clean, to limpiar
cleaner's shop tintorería *f.*
clearly claro

climate clima *m.*
climb, to ascender
clinic clínica *f.*
close junto
close, to cerrar
closed cerrado,-a
closet armario *m.*
cloth paño *m.*
clothes ropa *f.*
cloudy nublado,-a
club casino, club *m.*
clutch embrague *m.*
coal carbón *m.*
coast costa *f.*
coat chaqueta *f.* saco *m.*
cock gallo *m.*
cock fights pelea de gallos *f.*
cock pit gallera *f.*
cockroach cucaracha *f.*
cocktail coctel *m.*
cocoa cacao *m.*
cocoanut coco *m.*
coffee café *m.*
  ... with milk café con leche
  ... pot cafetera *f.*
cold, to get enfriarse
cold frío,-a
cold (illness) resfrío, resfriado
cold, I am tengo frío
cold, to catch resfriarse
collar cuello *m.*
colony colonia *f.*
color color *m.*
comb peine *m.*
come in, to entrar
come, to venir
come down, to bajar
comfortable comfortable,
  cómodo,-a
commercial comercial
company compañía *f.*
comparison comparación *f.*
complain, to reclamar
complaint reclamación *f.*
concern firma *f.*
concerning acerca de,
  tocante a
concert concierto *m.*
conductor conductor *m.*

confetti confeti *m.*
congratulate, to congratular
consist, to consistir
construct, to construir
consultation consulta *f.*
contract, to contraer
contrary contrario,-a
convenient conveniente
conversation conversación *f.*
convince, to convencer
cook cocinero,-a
cook, to cocinar
cookie galleta *f.*
cool fresco,-a
copper cobre *m.*
copy copia *f.*
cordial cordial
corkscrew sacacorchos
corn maíz *m.*
   . . . ear of mazorca *f.*
corner esquina *f.*
correct correcto,-a
correction corrección *f.*
correspondence
   correspondencia *f.*
corridor corredor *m.*
cosmetic cosmético *m.*
cost, to costar
cotton algodón *m.*
cough tos *f.*
count, to contar
country campo, país *m.*
couple par *m.*
course, of por supuesto
courteous cortés
courtesy cortesía *f.*
cousin primo,-a
cover, to cubrir
cracker galleta *f.*
crazy loco,-a
cream crema *f.*
credential credencial *f.*
credit crédito *m.*
criminal criminal
cry, to llorar
crystal cristal *m.*
Cuban cubano,-a
cucumber pepino *m.*
cuff puño *m.*

cup taza *f.*
curtain cortina *f.*
custard natilla *f.*
cutlet filete *m.*
customhouse aduana *f.*
cut, to cortar

D

daily diario *m.*
dance baile *m.*
dance, to bailar
danger peligro
dangerous peligroso,-a
dark oscuro-a
   to become . . . anochecer
darkness oscuridad *f.*
date (appointment) cita *f.*,
   compromiso *m.*
   (fruit) dátil *m.*
   (of calendar) fecha *f.*
daughter hija
day día *m.*
   . . . after tomorrow pasado
      mañana
   . . . before yesterday
      anteayer
daybreak amanecer *m.*
December diciembre *m.*
decide, to decidir
decision decisión *f.*
declaration declaración *f.*
decorate, to decorar
deduction deducción *f.*
deer ciervo *m.*
defect defecto *m.*
defective defectivo,-a
defend, to defender
degree grado *m.*
delicious delicioso,-a
deliver, to entregar
delivery entrega *f.*
demand, to exigir
dentist dentista *m.f.*
departure salida
deposit, to depositar
descend, to descender
describe, to describir
description descripción *f.*
desire deseo *m.*; gana *f.*

desk escritorio *m.*
dessert postre *m.*
detain, to detener
detest, to detestar
detour desvío *m.*
diamond diamante *m.*
dictionary diccionario *m.*
difference diferencia *f.*
different diferente
difficult difícil
difficulty dificultad *f.*
digestible digestible
digestion digestión *f.*
dine, to cenar
dining room comedor *m.*
direct directo,-a
direction dirección *f.*
director director,-a
dirty sucio,-a
directory directorio *m.*
dish plato *m.*
disagreeable desagradable
disappear, to desaparecer
disastrous desastroso,-a
discount descuento *m.*
discover, to descubrir
discuss, to discutir
discussion discusión *f.*
disobey, to desobedecer
distance distancia *f.*
distribute, to distribuír
divide, to dividir
dizziness mareo *m.*
doctor doctor,-a; médico,a
dog perro *m.*
dollar dólar *m.*
donkey burro,-a
door puerta *f.*
  . . . (car) portezuela *f.*
dot punto *m.*
double doble
doubt duda *f.*
doubt, to dudar
dove paloma *f.*
dozen docena *f.*
draft (financial) giro *m.*
  letra *f.*
  (current) corriente *f.*
dream sueño *m.*

dream, to soñar
dress vestido *m.*
dress, to vestir
dress (yourself), to vestirse
dressing (sauce) salsa *f.*
dressmaker modista *f.*
drink, to beber, tomar
drive, to manejar
driver conductor *m*
drugstore botica, droguería *f.*
drunk, to get emborracharse
dry, to (yourself) secarse
duck pato *m.*
dump, to echar
durable durable, duradero,-a
during durante
duty deber *m.*
  . . . (tax) impuesto *m.*

E

each cada
eagle águila *m.*
ear oreja *f.*
earlier más temprano
early temprano
earth tierra *f.*
ease facilidad *f.*
east oriente *m.*
Easter Pascua *f.*
easy fácil
eat, to comer
effective efectivo,-a
egg huevo *m.*
  . . . fried huevo frito
  . . . hard boiled huevo duro
  . . . soft boiled huevo pasado
    por agua
eight ocho
eighteen dieciocho
eighty ochenta
elbow codo *m.*
electric eléctrico,-a
electricity electricidad *f.*
elegant elegante
elephant elefante *m.*
elevator elevador, ascensor *m.*
eleven once
embark, to embarcar
embroidery bordado *m.*

emergency emergencia *f.*
encounter encuentro *m.*
encounter, to encontrar
end fin *m.*
engineer ingeniero *m.*
enough bastante, suficiente
   ... that is basta
enter, to entrar
entertain, to entretener
entertainment diversión *f.*
enthusiasm entusiasmo *m.*
enthusiastic entusiástico
envelope cubierta *f.* sobre *m.*
equal igual
equivalent equivalente
errand mandado *m.*
error error *m.*
essential esencial
establish, to establecer
evade, to evadir
eve víspera *f.*
evening noche *f.*
everything todo
exact exacto,-a
exactly exactamente, en punto
exaggerate, to exagerar
exaggeration exageración *f.*
examine, to examinar
excavation excavación *f.*
except excepto, menos
excessive excesivo,-a
exchange cambio *m.*
excuse, to dispensar
   ... me excúseme,
     dispénseme
exhibition exhibición *f.*
existence existencia *f.*
exit salida
expensive caro,-a
expect, to esperar
expected esperado
experience experiencia *f.*
explain, to explicar
export, to exportar
express, to expresar
exterior exterior

F

fabric tela *f.*

face cara *f.*
facial facial
factory fábrica *f.*
fail, to fracasar
failure fracaso *m.*
fair justo,-a
fall, to caer
family familia *f.*
famous famoso,-a
fan aficionado,-a
far lejos
farm granja *f.*
farmer agricultor
fashion moda *f.*
fast pronto
fat gordo,-a
father padre *m.*
favor favor *m.*
favorite predilecto,-a
fear, to temer
fear miedo *m.*
feast festividad, fiesta *f.*
February, febrero *m.*
feel, to sentir
felt fieltro *m.*
fervor fervor
festival festival *m.*
fever fiebre *f.*
fifteen quince
fifty cincuenta *m.*
fig higo *m.*
film película *f.*
film roll rollo *m.*
finally finalmente, en fin
find, to encontrar
find out, to enterarse
finger dedo *m.*
finish, to terminar
finished terminado,-a
firm firma *f.*
first primero,-a
first class primera clase
fish pescado *m.*
fish, to pescar
fit, to ajustar
five cinco *m.*
fixed compuesto,-a
flame llama *f.*
flannel franela *f.*

flight vuelo *m.*
float, to flotar
floor piso *m.*
flower flor *f.*
fly mosco *m.*
fly, to volar
food alimento *m.*
foot pie *m.*
for para, por
foreign extranjero,-a
foreigner extranjero,-a
forget, to olvidar
fork tenedor *m.*
form, to formar
formal formal
fort fuerte *m.*
fortune fortuna *f.*
forty cuarenta
forward adelante
fountain fuente *f.*
four cuatro
fourteen catorce
fox zorro *m.*
free de balde, gratis
freeze, to helar
French francés,-sa
frequently frecuentemente
fresh fresco
Friday viernes *m.*
fried frito,-a
friend amigo,-a
frightened, to get asustarse
from desde, de
front, in al frente
frost helada *f.*
frozen congelado,-a
fruit fruta *f.*
fry, to freír
funeral funeral *m.*
funny chistoso,-a
fur piel *f.*
furnished amueblado,-a
furniture mobiliario *m.*

G

gamble, to jugar
game juego *m.*
garage garage *m.*
garden jardín *m.*

gardener hortelano,-a
garlic ajo *m.*
gas station estación de
   gasolina *f.*
gasoline gasolina *f.*
general general *m.*
generator generador *m.*
gentleman señor, caballero
get rid of, to deshacerse
get off or down, to bajar
gin ginebra *f.*
girl niña, muchacha
give, to dar
   dé (imp.)
   ... it to me démelo
glad, to be alegrarse
glove guante *m.*
go, to ir
   ... in, to entrar
   ... to bed, to acostarse
   ... down to descender
   let's ... vámonos
goat cabra *f.*
God Dios
gold oro *m.*
golf golf *m.*
good bueno,-a; buen
   ... afternoon buenas tardes
   ... luck buena suerte
   ... morning buenos días
   ... night buenas noches
goods artículos
goose ganso *m.*
government gobierno *m.*
graceful gracioso,-a
gracious! ¡caramba!
grain grano *m.*
granddaughter nieta *f.*
grandfather abuelo *m.*
grandmother abuela *f.*
grandson nieto *m.*
grape uva *f.*
gray gris *m.*
green verde
greet, to saludar
greeting saludo *m.*
groan quejido *m.*
gross gruesa *f.*
ground suelo *m.*

ground floor piso bajo
grow, to crecer
growth crecimiento *m.*
guest invitado,-a
guitar guitarra *f.*

H

hair pelo *m.*
half medio,-a, mitad
hall corredor *m.*
ham jamón *m.*
hand mano *f.*
hand (of a watch)
    manecilla *f.*
handbag cartera *f.*
handkerchief pañuelo *m.*
handsome guapo,-a
happiness felicidad,
    ventura *f.*
happy contento,-a
hard duro,-a
hare liebre *f.*
harvest cosecha *f.*
haste prisa *f.*
hat sombrero *m.*
hat store sombrerería *f.*
hate, to odiar
hatred odio *m.*
have, to tener
hay heno *m.*
hazelnut avellana *f.*
he él
head cabeza *f.*
health salud *f.*
hear, to oír
hearing oído *m.*
heat calor *m.*
heating calefacción *f.*
heel tacón *m.*
hen gallina *f.*
here aquí
hiccough hipo *m.*
high alto,-a; elevado,-a
highway carretera *f.*
hire, to alquilar
history historia *f.*
holiday fiesta, *f.*
home hogar *m.*
honey miel de abejas

honeymoon luna de miel *f.*
honor honor *m.*
hope esperanza *f.*
hope, to esperar
horse caballo *m.*
horse race carrera de caballos
hospital hospital *m.*
hospitality hospitalidad *f.*
hot caliente
    ... I am tengo calor
hour hora *f.*
house casa *f.*
how cómo
    ... are you?
        ¿cómo está usted?
    ... far is it?
        ¿Qué tan lejos es?
    ... many cuántos
    ... much cuánto
humidity humedad *f.*
humor humor *m.*
hundred ciento
hunger hambre *m.*
hungry, I am tengo hambre
hurry, to apurarse
    ... up! apúrese!
hurt, to doler
    ... yourself, to lastimarse
husband esposo, marido *m.*

I

I yo
ice hielo *m.*
ice cream helado *m.*
idea idea *f.*
if si
ignorance ignorancia *f.*
ignorant ignorante
ill mal
    very ... grave
illegal ilegal
illustration ilustración *f.*
imagination imaginación *f.*
imitation imitación *f.*
immense inmenso,-a
impatience impaciencia *f.*
import, to importar
important importante
impossible imposible

impossibility imposibilidad *f.*
in en
incidentally por cierto
include, to incluír
income renta *f.*
incompetent incompetente
incorrect incorrecto,-a
indeed en verdad
independence
   independencia *f.*
indigestion indigestión *f.*
indisposed indispuesto,-a
industrial industrial
infection infección *f.*
influence influencia *f.*
inform, to informar
inhabitant habitante
initial inicial
ink tinta *f.*
inoculate, to inocular
insect insecto *m.*
inside adentro, dentro
install, to instalar
instant instante *m.*
insult insulto *m.*
insurance seguro
intelligent inteligente
interior interior
international internacional
interrupt, to interrumpir
intimate íntimo,-a
introduce, to presentar
introduction introducción
invitation invitación *f.*
invite, to invitar
invoice factura *f.*
iron, to planchar
is es
it is es
itinerary itinerario *m.*

J

jacket chaqueta *f.*
jail cárcel *f.*
jam (tight spot) aprieto
January enero *m.*
jealousy celos *m.*
jest burla *f.*
jewel joya *f.*

jewelry store joyería *f.*
Jewish judío
joke chiste *m.*
journal diario *m.*
joy gozo *m.*
judgment juicio *m.*
juice jugo *m.*
July julio *m.*
jump, to saltar
June junio *m.*
just justo,-a
justice justicia *f.*

K

keep out! prohibida la
   entrada!
key llave *f.*
kilogram kilo *m.*
kind clase *f.*
kitchen cocina *f.*
knife cuchillo *m.*
knock on the door, to tocar
know, to saber
know, to (people, places)
   conocer

L

laborious laborioso,-a
lace encaje *m.*
lack, to faltar
ladder escalera *f.*
lake lago *m.*
lamb cordero *m.*
lamp lámpara *f.*
lamp shade pantalla *f.*
language idioma *m.*
large grande
lark alondra *f.*
last último,-a; postrero,-a
   ... **night** anoche
   at ... al fin, por fin
   to ... durar
lately últimamente
later más tarde, luego
laugh, to reír
laughter risa *f.*
laughter, burst of carcajada
laundry lavandería *f.*
lavatory baño *m.*

lawyer abogado *m.*
lazy perezoso,-a
leaf hoja *f.*
learn, to aprender
lease, to arrendar
leather piel *f.*
leave, to dejar, salir
left izquierda *f.*
leg pierna *f.*
legal legal
lemon limón *m.*
lemonade limonada *f.*
lend, to prestar
lentil lenteja *f.*
less menos
lesson lección *f.*
let, to dejar
letter carta, letra *f.*
lettuce lechuga *f.*
library bilioteca *f.*
lie mentira *f.*
lie, to mentir
lie down, to acostar
life vida *f.*
lift, to levantar
light luz *f.*
light, to encender
lightning relámpago *m.*
like, to gustar
lily lirio *m.*
lime lima *f.*
linen lino *m.*
lion león *m.*
list lista *f.*
listen! ¡oíga!
little poco,-a; menudo,-a;
   chiquito,-a
live, to vivir
living room sala *f.*
lobby vestíbulo *m.*
local local
location sitio *m.*
lock in, to encerrar
locker gaveta *f.*
long largo,-a
   ... too muy largo,-a
look! ¡míre!
lose, to perder
lottery lotería *f.*

loud alto,-a
love amor *m.*
love, to querer
low bajo,-a
lubrication lubricación *f.*
lubricant lubricante *m.*
lubricate, to lubricar
luck suerte *f.*
lunch almuerzo *m.*
lunch (to have) almorzar
luxury lujo *m.*

M

machine máquina *f.*
machinery maquinaria *f.*
maid criada *f.*
maid, room camarera *f.*
mail correo *m.*
mailbox buzón *m.*
major mayor
make, to hacer, realizar
man hombre
manage, to manejar
manner modo *m.*
mansion mansión *f.*
many muchos,-as
many, as, so tantos, as
map mapa *m.*
March marzo *m.*
market plaza *f.*
market place mercado *m.*
marmalade mermelada *f.*
match fósforo *m.*
mattress colchón *m.*
May mayo *m.*
maybe tal vez
mayor alcalde *m.*
me mí
measure, to medir
meat carne *f.*
mechanic mecánico,-a
medicine medicina *f.*
meet, to encontrar
melon melón *m.*
melt, to derretir
memory memoria *f.*
mend, to remendar
menu menú *m.*
merchandise mercancía *f.*

merchant comerciante *m.*
metal metal *m.*
Mexican mexicano,-a
midday mediodía *m.*
middle medio *m.*
midnight medianoche *f.*
milk leche *f.*
mine mío,-a
mine mina, *f.*
mineral mineral *m.*
minute minuto *m.*
mistake, to make a
  equivocarse
mix, to revolver
modern moderno,-a
moment momento *m.*
Monday lunes *m.*
money dinero *m.*
  paper ... billete
monkey mono *m.*
month mes *m.*
moon luna *f.*
more más
morning mañana *f.*
moreover además
mother madre
motor motor *m.*
motorist motorista *m., f.*
mouse ratón *m.*
move, to mudar, mover
movie screen pantalla *f.*
moving moviendo
moving picture película
much mucho,-a
much, as, so tanto,-a
  too ... demasiado
mud lodo, fango *m.*
mule mula *f.*
municipal municipal
mural mural
museum museo *m.*
mushroom seta *f.*
music música *f.*
mustard mostaza *f.*
mutton carnero *m.*
my mi, mis
myself mí

N

name nombre *m.*
napkin servilleta *f.*
narrow estrecho, angosto,-a
nation nación *f.*
national nacional
nationality nacionalidad *f.*
native nativo,-a
natural natural
naturally naturalmente
navy marina *f.*
near cerca, junto
  ... to cerca de
necessary necesario,-a
necessity necesidad *f.*
neck cuello *m.*
necktie corbata *f.*
need, to necesitar
needle aguja *f.*
needlework costura *f.*
negative negativo
negligent negligente
neighbor vecino,-a
neither ningún, ninguno,-a
  tampoco, ni
nephew sobrino *m.*
nervous nervioso,-a
never nunca, jamás
new nuevo,-a
New Year Año Nuevo
news noticias *f.*
newspaper periódico *m.*
newsreel noticiario *m.*
next próximo,-a
niece sobrina *f.*
night noche *f.*
nine nueve *m.*
ninety noventa
nineteen diecinueve
no no
noble noble
nobody nadie
noon mediodía *m.*
no one ninguno,-a
nor ni
north norte
North America Norte
  América

North American
 norteamericano,-a
note nota *f.*
notebook cuaderno *m.*
note, to notar
notice, to notar
nothing nada
November noviembre *m.*
now ahora
 right . . . ahora
number número *m.*
numerous numeroso,-a
nut nuez *f.*

O

oat avena *f.*
obtain, to obtener
occasion ocasión *f.*
occupation ocupación *f.*
occupy, to ocupar
October octubre *m.*
occur, to ocurrir
oculist oculista *m.*
odd raro,-a
of de
offend, to ofender
offended ofendido,-a
offensive ofensivo,-a
offer, to ofrecer
office oficina *f.*
official oficial
often a menudo
oil aceite *m.*
old viejo,-a
olive aceituna *f.*
omelet tortilla *f.*
on en, sobre
once una vez
one uno,-a
one way una vía
onion cebolla *f.*
open abierto,-a
open, to abrir
opera ópera *f.*
operation operación *f.*
operator operador
opinion opinión *f.*
opposite al frente
or o

orange naranja *f.*
 . . . juice jugo de naranja
orchard huerta *f.*
orchestra orquesta *f.*
orchid orquídea *f.*
order orden *f.*
order, to pedir
ordinarily generalmente
ordinary ordinario,-a
original original
ornament adorno *m.*
other otro,-a
ounce onza *f.*
our, ours nuestro,-a
ourselves nosotros,-as
out of order descompuesto,-a
outside exterior, fuera, afuera,
oven horno *m.*
overcoat abrigo *m.*
overturn, to volcar
own propio,-a
owner dueño,-a
ox buey
oyster ostra *f.*

P

park, to estacionar
parrot loro *m.*
patience paciencia *f.*
patient paciente
patriotic patriótico,-a
pattern patrón *m.*
package paquete *m.*
paint, to pintar
painting pintura *f.*
pair par *m.*
palace palacio *m.*
palm tree palma, palmera *f.*
paper papel *m.*
park parque *m.*
parking parqueadero *m.*
pass, to pasar
past pasado,-a
paste pasta *f.*
pay, to pagar
payment pago *m.*
peaceful tranquilo,-a
peach melocotón *m.*
pear pera *f.*

peas guisantes *m.*
peasant peón *m.*
pen pluma *f.*
pencil lápiz *m.*
penicillin penicilina *f.*
pension pensión *f.*
people gente *f.*
pepper pimienta *f.*
per cent por ciento
percentage tanto por ciento
perfect perfecto,-a
perform, to realizar
perfume perfume *m.*
perhaps quizá, quizás, acaso
permanent permanente *f.*
permanent wave permanente
permitted permitido,-a
person, in personalmente
personal personal
personally personalmente
perspire, to sudar
persuade, to persuadir
peso peso *m.*
petroleum petróleo *m.*
phonograph fonógrafo *f.*
phonograph record disco *m.*
photograph fotografía *f.*
photograph, to fotografiar
pick up, to levantar
picture pintura *f.*
    cuadro *m.*
    retrato (portrait) *m.*
pie pastel *m.*
pier muelle *m.*
pig cerdo *m.*
pill píldora *f.*
pillow almohada *f.*
pilot piloto *m.*
pine tree pino *m.*
pineapple piña *f.*
pipe pipa *f.*
pitcher jarra *f.*
place sitio, lugar *m.*
plan plan *m.*
plant planta *f.*
plate plato *m.*
platter fuente *f.*
play, to jugar
play, to (instrument) tocar

pleasant agradable
pleasure gusto, placer *m.*
plum ciruela *f.*
pocket bolsillo *m.*
point punto *m.*
point, to señalar
policeman policía *m.*
politics política *f.*
poor pobre
popular popular
poppy amapola *f.*
pork puerco *m.*
    ...**chop** chuleta de cerdo
port puerto *m.*
position posición *f.*
positive positivo,-a
possible posible
possibly posiblemente
postal postal
potato papa *f.*
pour, to echar
powder polvo *m.*
    polvos (cosmetic)
practice, to practicar
practical práctico,-a
precious precioso,-a
prefer, to preferir
preferred predilecto,-a
prepare, to preparar
prescription receta *f.*
present presente, regalo (gift) *m.*
present, to presentar
pretty bonito,-a
price precio *m.*
principal principal
print, to imprimir
prize premio *m.*
probably probablemente
proceed, to proceder
produce, to producir
product producto *m.*
profession profesión *f.*
profit ganancia *f.*
program programa *m.*
progress progreso *m.*
progress, to progresar
prohibit, to prohibir
promise, to prometer
pronounce, to pronunciar

pronunciation pronunciación f.
proof prueba f.
propeller hélice f.
proper propio,-a
protest, to protestar
protection protección f.
Protestant protestante
prove, to probar
province provincia f.
public público,-a
pulse pulso m.
pumpkin calabaza f.
punctual puntual
purchase compra f.
purse bolso,-a
put, to poner
... on, to ponerse
... to bed, to acostar
... out, to apagar, echar

Q

quantity cantidad f.
quarter cuarto m.
quarterly trimestre
question pregunta f.
quick aprisa
quotation cotización f.

R

rabbit conejo m.
racial racial
radiator radiador m.
radio radio m.
radish rábano m.
railroad ferrocarril m.
railroad car coche m.
rain lluvia f.
rain, to llover
raincoat impermeable m.; gabardina f.
raise, to levantar, alzar
raisin pasa f.
ranch rancho m.
rapid rápido,-a
rapidly rápidamente
rare raro,-a
raspberry frambuesa f.
rat rata f.

raw crudo,-a
rayon rayón m.
razor navaja de afeitar
razor blade cuchilla f.
read, to leer
ready listo,-a
reality realidad, verdad f.
realize, to realizar
really? ¿de veras?
reason razón f.
receipt recibo m.
receive, to recibir
recent reciente
recognize, to reconocer
recommend, to recomendar
recommendation recomendación f.
recreation recreación f.
red colorado, rojo,-a
red snapper pargo m., huachinango m. (Mex.)
reduce, to reducir
reflector reflector m.
refresh, to refrescar
refrigeration refrigeración f.
refrigerator refrigeradora f.
region región f.
register, to registrar, matricular
registration registración, matriculación f.
regularity regularidad f.
relation relación f.
relative pariente, m.
remain, to quedarse
remember, to recordar
remind, to acordar
rent renta f.
rent, to arrendar
repair, to componer
repeat, to repetir
repair, to reparar
require, to requerir
resemble, to parecerse
residential residencial
respectable respetable
responsible responsable
rest, to descansar
restaurant restaurante m.

restriction restricción f.
return, to regresar, devolver, volver
reunion reunión f.
rib costilla f.
ribbon cinta f.
rice arroz m.
ride, to montar
ride, to take a pasear
ridiculous ridículo,-a
right derecha f. (direction), correcto
rise, to ascender, subir
river río m.
road camino m.
roadmap guía del viajero
roast, to asar
roast beef rosbif m.
roasted asado,-a
rob, to robar
robbery robo m.
romantic romántico,-a
room pieza, habitación, f.; cuarto, m.
roomy espacioso,-a
rosary rosario m.
rose rosa f.
route ruta f.
rubber goma, caucho
rug alfombra f.
rum ron m.
rumba rumba f.
rural rural
rumor rumor m.
Russian ruso,-a
rye centeno m.

S

sail, to embarcar
safe seguro,-a
salad ensalada f.
salary salario m.
salt sal f.
salty salado,-a
same mismo,-a
sample muestra f.
sandwich sandwich m.
sardine sardina f.
satisfy, to satisfacer

Saturday sábado m.
sauce salsa f.
save, to salvar
say, to decir
scarcely apenas
school colegio m.; escuela f.
scissors tijeras f.
scorpion alacrán m.
scrape lío m.
scratch, to rascar
scream grito m.
scream, to gritar
sculpture escultura f.
seal sello m.
seasick, to get marearse
season estación f.
seat asiento m.
second segundo,-a
second class segunda clase
secretary secretario,-a
section sección f.
sedative sedativo m.
see, to ver
seem, to parecer
seldom rara vez
select, to seleccionar
selection selección f.
self starter arranque automático m.
sell, to vender
send, to mandar
sensation sensación f.
September septiembre m.
serve, to servir
service servicio m.
seven siete
seventeen diecisiete
seventy setenta
several varios,-as
sew, to coser
shade sombra f.
shave, to afeitar
she ella
sheep oveja f.
sheet sábana, hoja f.
shepherd pastor m.
shipment despacho, envío, m.
shirt camisa f.
shoe zapato m.

shoestore zapatería f.
shop almacén m.
short corto,-a
   too ... muy corto,-a
shoulder hombro m.
shout, to gritar
shovel pala f.
show, to enseñar, mostrar,
   señalar
shrimp camarón m.
shut, to cerrar
sick enfermo,-a
   I am ... estoy enfermo
sickness enfermedad f.
get sick, to enfermarse
sidewalk acera f.
sigh suspiro m.
sight vista f.
sign, to firmar
sign letrero m.
silence silencio m.
silk seda f.
simple simple
simplicity simplicidad f.
since desde, pues
sincerity sinceridad f.
sing, to cantar
single solo, simple, único
sink fregadero m.
sister hermana f.
sister-in-law cuñada f.
sit, to sentar
sit down, to sentarse
situate, to situar
situation situación f.
six seis
sixteen dieciséis m.
sixty sesenta
size talla f.
sky cielo m.
sleep, to dormir
sleep, to go to dormirse
sleeve manga f.
slip, to resbalar
slipper zapatilla f.
slow despacio, lento
small pequeño, chiquito,-a
   too... muy pequeño,-a;
   muy chiquito,-a

smell, to oler
smile, to sonreír
smoke, to fumar
sneeze estornudo m.
snore, to roncar
snow nieve f.
snow, to nevar
so (thus) así
   ... long hasta luego
   ... that conque
soap jabón m.
soap dish jabonera f.
sob sollozo m.
sociable sociable
social social
society sociedad f.
sock calcetín m.
sofa sofá m.
soft suave, blando,-a
soft drink bebida gaseosa
sole suela f.
solution solución f.
some unos,-as
somebody alguien
someone alguno,-a
something algo
son hijo
song canto m.; canción f.
soon pronto
sorry, to be sentir
   I am ... lo siento
soup sopa f.
south sur m.
South America Sur América
souvenir recuerdo
sow, to sembrar
sowing siembra
space espacio m.
spacious espacioso,-a
Spain España f.
Spaniard español,-a
Spanish español,-a
spark plug bujía f.
sparrow gorrión m.
speak, to hablar
special especial
specially especialmente
speech discurso m.
speed velocidad f.

spicy picante
spinach espinaca f.
sponge esponja f.
spoon cuchara f.
spoonful cucharada f.
spring primavera f.
square plaza f.; cuadrado,-a
squirrel ardilla f.
stadium estadio m.
staircase escalera f.
stairs escalones m.
stamp sello m.; estampilla f.
stand up, to pararse
state estado m.
station estación f.
station wagon camioneta f.
stationery store papelería f.
statue estatua f.
stay, to quedarse
steak bisté m.
steal, to robar
steam vapor m.
steamship vapor m.
steps escalones m.
stew guisado m.
stockings medias f. pl.
stomach estómago m.
stone piedra f.
stop! ¡pare!, ¡alto!
stop, to parar
store tienda f.
storm tormenta f.
story cuento m.
stove estufa f.
straight, straight ahead
   derecho,-a
strange extraño,-a
straw paja f.
strawberry fresa f.
street calle f.
string bean ejote m.
student estudiante
stupid estúpido,-a
style moda f.; estilo m.
suburb suburbio m.
success éxito m.
successively sucesivamente
sudden de pronto, de repente
sufficient suficiente, bastante

sugar azúcar m.
sugar bowl azucarero m.
suit traje m.
suitcase maleta f.
summer verano m.
sun sol m.
Sunday domingo m.
supper cena f.
supper, to have cenar
supposed supuesto
sure cierto,-a
surprise, to sorprender
swallow golondrina f.
sweater suéter m.
sweep, to barrer
sweet dulce
sweet potato batata f.
swim, to nadar
swimming pool piscina f.
system sistema m.

T

table mesa f.
tablecloth mantel m.
tailor sastre m.
tailor shop sastrería f.
take, to llevar, tomar
take leave, to despedirse
tall alto,-a
tango tango m.
tank tanque m.
tassel espiga f.
taste gusto m.
taste, to probar, gustar
tasteless desabrido,-a
tea té m.
teach, to enseñar
teacher maestro,-a
tear lágrima f.
tear, to romper
teaspoon cucharita f.
telegram telegrama m.
telegraph operator telegrafista
telephone teléfono m.
television televisión f.
tell, to decir
   ...me dígame
temper genio m.

temperature fiebre,
   temperatura *f.*
ten diez *m.*
tender tierno,-a
tenth décimo,-a
terrace terraza *f.*
terrible terrible
test, to probar
thank you gracias
that ese, eso,-a, aquel,-la, que,
   quien, cual
that way por allá
the el, la, los, las
   about ... del
   at ... al
   from ... del
   of ... del
   to ... al
theft robo *m.*
then entonces, luego
there ahí, allí, allá
   ... is, are hay
these estos, estas
thin delgado,-a
thing cosa *f.*
think, I yo creo, yo pienso
think, to creer, pensar
third, one tercio
thirsty, I am tengo sed
thirteen trece
thirty treinta
this este, esta
   ... one éste, ésta
   ... way por aquí
thought pensamiento *m.*
thousand mil
thread hilo *m.*
three tres
thunder trueno *m.*
Thursday jueves *m.*
ticket boleto, billete,
   pasaje *m.*
tidy aseado,-a
tiger tigre *m.*
tight apretado estrecho,-a
tile mosaico *m.*
time tiempo, vez
   in, on ... a tiempo
   to have a good ... divertirse

times veces
tire llanta *f.*
tired cansado,-a
timetable itinerario,
   horario
tin estaño *m.*
tip propina *f.*
tired, to get cansarse
to para, a
toast tostada *f.*
toast, to tostar
tobacco tabaco *m.*
today hoy
together juntos,-as
tomato tomate *m.*
tomorrow mañana *f.*
tongue lengua *f.*
tonight esta noche
tooth diente *m.*
toothbrush cepillo de dientes
torrent torrente *m.*
toss, to echar
total total *m.*
touch, to tocar
tourist turista, viajero
toward hacia
towel toalla *f.*
town pueblo *m.*
toy juguete *m.*
traffic tráfico *m.*
train tren *m.*
transaction transacción *f.*
translate, to traducir
transparent transparente
transport, to transportar
travel, to viajar
traveler viajero,-a
travelers check cheque de viajero
tray bandeja *f.*
tree árbol *m.*
trimming adorno *m.*
trip viaje *m.*
trivial trivial
tropical tropical
tropics trópico *m.*
trouble dificultad *f.*; lío *m.*
trousers pantalones *m.*
trout trucha
truck camión *m.*

trunk baúl *m.*
truth veras, verdad *f.*
try it on mídaselo
try to, to tratar de
Tuesday martes *m.*
turkey pavo *m.*
turn off the light, to apagar
turn over, to volcar
turnip nabo *m.*
twelve doce
twenty veinte
twenty-five veinticinco
two dos
throw, to echar
type tipo *m.*
typewriter máquina de escribir
typical típico,-a

U

ugliness fealdad *f.*
ugly feo,-a
ultramarine ultramarino,-a
umbrella paraguas *m.*
uncertainty duda *f.*
uncle tío *m.*
under debajo, bajo
undershirt camiseta *f.*
understand, to comprender, entender
underwear ropa interior
undress, to desvestirse
until hasta
    . . . **we meet again** hasta la vista
unwrap, to desenvolver
up to hasta
up, to go subir
upon sobre
urgent urgente
us nos, nosotros,-as
used to be era
utility utilidad *f.*

V

vain, in en balde
value valor, importe *m.*
vaseline vaselina *f.*
veal ternera *f.*

vegetable legumbre *f.*
vehicle vehículo *m.*
velvet terciopelo *m.*
ventilate, to ventilar
ventilator ventilador *m.*
vertical vertical
very muy
    . . . **well** muy bien
vest chaleco *m.*
Viennese vienés,-a
view vista *f.*
vinegar vinagre *m.*
violet violeta *f.*
visit visita *f.*
visit, to visitar
vitamin vitamina *f.*
vocabulary vocabulario *m.*

W

wage pago, sueldo, jornal
waist cintura, talle *m.*
waistline cintura *f.*
wait, to esperar
waited esperado
waiter camarero,-a
wake up, to despertar
walk, to caminar, andar
walk, to take a pasear, caminar
wall pared *f.*
wallet cartera
waltz vals *m.*
want, to querer
warm caloroso, caliente
was era
was, there había, hubo
wash basin lavabo *m.*
wash, to lavar
    . . . **to (yourself)** bañarse
watch reloj
watchmaker relojero *m.*
watch shop relojería *f.*
water agua *m.*
watermelon sandía *f.*
waterproof impermeable *m.*
wave ola *f.*
we nosotros,-as
weakness debilidad *f.*
wear, to llevar

Wednesday miércoles *m.*
week semana *f.*
  by the ... por semana
weight peso *m.*
weigh, to pesar
weigh, to (yourself) pesarse
well bien
  ... done bien asado
were era
were, there había, hubo
west occidente *m.*
West Indies Antillas
what? ¿qué?
whatever cualquiera
wheat trigo m.
wheel rueda *f.*
when cuando
whenever siempre que
where donde
which que, cuál,-es
whip látigo *m.*
white blanco,-a
who? ¿quién?
whoever quienquiera
wide amplio, ancho,-a
wife esposa *f.*
will voluntad *f.*
wind viento *m.*
window ventana *f.*
windshield parabrisa *m.*
windshield wiper
  limpiavidrios
wine vino *m.*
winter invierno *m.*
wish, to desear
with con
with me conmigo

within dentro de
without sin, fuera
witness testigo *m.*
wolf lobo *m.*
woman mujer
wonderful admirable
wood madera *f.*
woods bosque *m.*
wool lana *f.*
word palabra *f.*
work trabajo *m.*
work, to trabajar
workman trabajador
world mundo *m.*
worried preocupado,-a
worry, to preocupar
worse peor
wrap, to envolver
wrapped envuelto,-a
wrinkle arruga *f.*
write, to escribir
writing escribiendo
written escrito

Y

yawn bostezo *m.*
year año *m.*
yellow amarillo,-a
yes sí
yesterday ayer
yet todavía, aun
young joven
youth juventud *f.*

Z

zero cero *m.*